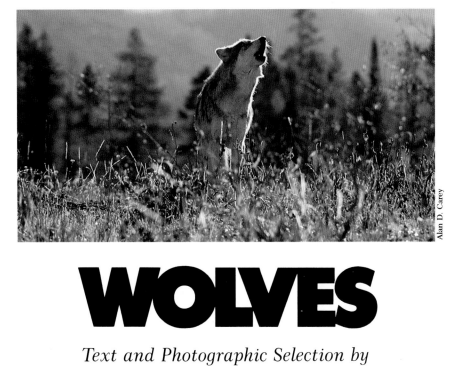

Alan D. Carey

WOLVES

Text and Photographic Selection by

CANDACE SAVAGE

Foreword by L. David Mech

Sierra Club Books
San Francisco

The Sierra Club, founded in 1892 by John Muir, has devoted itself to the study and protection of the earth's scenic and ecological resources—mountains, wetlands, woodlands, wild shores and rivers, deserts and plains. The publishing program of the Sierra Club offers books to the public as a nonprofit educational service in the hope that they may enlarge the public's understanding of the Club's basic concerns. The point of view expressed in each book, however, does not necessarily represent that of the Club. The Sierra Club has some sixty chapters coast to coast, in Canada, Hawaii, and Alaska. For information about how you may participate in its programs to preserve wilderness and the quality of life, please address inquiries to Sierra Club, 730 Polk Street, San Francisco, CA 94109.

Originally published in Canada by Douglas & McIntyre Ltd., 1615 Venables Street, Vancouver, British Columbia, Canada V5L 2H1.

Library of Congress Cataloging-in-Publication Data

Savage, Candace Sherk, 1949-
    Wolves.

    Bibliography: p.
    1. Wolves.   1. Title.
QL737.C22S32   1989   599.74′442   88-18391
ISBN 0-87156-689-3

The following publishers have given permission to use quoted material:
From *Of Wolves and Men*, by Barry Lopez. Copyright © 1978 by Barry Holstun Lopez. Reprinted by permission of Charles Scribner's Sons, an imprint of Macmillan Publishing Company. From *Muskoxen of Polar Bear Pass*, by David R. Gray. Copyright © 1987 by David R. Gray. Reprinted by permission of Fitzhenry & Whiteside. From *Hunters in the Barrens*, by Georg Henriksen. Copyright © 1973 by the Institute of Social and Economic Research. Reprinted by permission of ISER Books, Institute of Social and Economic Research, Memorial University of Newfoundland. From *A Naturalist in Alaska*, by Adolph Murie. Copyright © 1961 by the Devin-Adair Company. Reprinted by permission of Devin-Adair Publishers. From *American*, by Frank B. Linderman. Copyright © 1930, 1972 by Frank B. Linderman. Reprinted by permission of Harper & Row Publishers, Inc.

Maps by Lisa Ireton
Typeset by The Typeworks
Printed and bound in Singapore by C. S. Graphics Pte. Ltd.
10   9   8   7   6   5   4   3   2   1

For Arthur, seven years after

CONTENTS

ACKNOWLEDGEMENTS

Writing is often thought of as solitary work: one mind facing the uncertainty of a blank page. But, in fact, most books are created by a community of skilled and committed people, and this volume is no exception.

I wish in particular to thank Douglas Heard and Mark Williams of the Northwest Territories Department of Renewable Resources in Yellowknife, for sharing their knowledge and their reference libraries and for taking me flying over what seemed like most of the western N.W.T. This project would scarcely have been possible without their help.

Appreciation is also due to Jane McHughen and Nora Russell of Western Producer Prairie Books, and to Valerie Ahwee of Douglas & McIntyre, who showed exceptional patience in collecting photographs for this book and assisting with the final selection. Thanks too to Terry Wolfe and John Poirier for their help.

In addition, I am deeply indebted to Richard Clarke, Rob Sanders and Diana Savage for their generous and unwavering support.

The manuscript was read during its preparation by Douglas Heard, Mark Williams, David Mech, Marilyn Sacks and Robert Janes, each of whom made valuable suggestions for its improvement. Any remaining errors or inadequacies in the text are the result of the author's inability to recognize good advice when it is offered.

F O R E W O R D

Thirty years ago, I started studying wolves. There had been only three or four detailed investigations then of these fascinating and magnificent creatures, and public sentiment reflected this dearth of knowledge. Wolves were definitely not popular. They had been exterminated from all of the forty-eight contiguous states except Minnesota and Isle Royale National Park. Minnesota still bountied them. Aerial wolf hunting was legal and popular throughout Canada and Alaska.

And everybody knew wolves were dangerous to human beings. When as a green, twenty-one-year-old graduate student I began the Isle Royale wolf study under the direction of Durward Allen, the National Park Service insisted I carry a sidearm. When I first watched from the air as a pack of fifteen wolves killed a moose, my pilot would not accompany me as I chased off the wolves from the ground so I could examine the kill. He was a wolf hunter, and he knew wolves were not to be trusted. Even ten years later when I placed my first radio-collars on wolves, my wolf trapper greatly exaggerated both the weight and ferocity of the animals.

I fear that in those days a book like this would neither have been possible nor popular.

But times do change, at least sometimes for the better. When I first began giving talks about wildlife, and was introduced as a wildlife ecologist, I invariably had to begin by explaining what ecology was. Now ecology is a household word. The new public awareness about the natural world affected wolves profoundly and paved the way for a book like this.

Minnesota discarded its wolf bounty in 1965. Canadian provinces gradually prohibited public aerial wolf hunting and restricted their harvest regulations. Alaska followed suit. The U.S. government placed the wolf in the contiguous forty-eight states on its Endangered Species list and protected it. And wolves themselves began responding. Minnesota wolves started recolonizing neighboring Wisconsin where they had been exterminated. British Columbia wolves are colonizing northwestern Montana.

Meanwhile, public attitudes towards wolves have changed dramatically. No doubt this change has come about because some of the wolf's most ardent haters have passed away, while their offspring have been much less vehement. However, in addition, much of the formerly neutral general public has become interested in the wolf and has been influenced not so much by personal prejudices as by knowledge of the animal. Much of this knowledge has come in the form of books like this that show the animal in its true perspective.

Documentation of this new attitude towards wolves can be found in Yale University professor Steven Kellert's 1985 study of Minnesotans. A startling 72 per cent of the residents of wolf range agreed with the statement, "To me, the timber wolf symbolizes the beauty and wonder of nature." Even Minnesota farmers, some of whom actually sustain livestock losses to wolves, showed surprising tolerance of the animal. Only 24 per cent of them agreed with the statement, "Timber wolves belong in places like Alaska, not in Minnesota."

Further evidence of a change in human attitudes towards wolves comes in the concrete form of an attempt to start to undo some of the damage our ancestors wreaked on the wolf population. In North Carolina, the U.S. Fish and Wildlife Service has reintroduced four pairs of the red wolf, close cousin to the gray wolf, into Alligator River National Wildlife Refuge, and the re-establishment appears to be quite successful at this writing. In addition, public calls have proliferated significantly for the reintroduction of the wolf into Yellowstone National Park, where it was foolishly exterminated fifty years ago. Congressman Wayne Owens of Utah has even introduced a bill into the U.S. Congress promoting wolf reintroduction into Yellowstone.

It is certainly true that in parts of Minnesota, Alaska and Canada there are still active wolf-control programs. However, these are either where wolves are preying on livestock or where their populations are high relative to prey sought by humans. In no case are such control programs being conducted where wolves are endangered. And the good news is that it is local control that is being practised, not extermination.

As a further reflection of the increasingly favorable attitude that humans are showing towards wolves is the production and display of the "Wolves and Humans" exhibit by the Science Museum of Minnesota. First displayed at the museum itself, and currently touring major museums in the U.S. and Canada, this exhibit has now been viewed by more than 1.5 million people. When it completes its tour, the exhibit is scheduled to become the corner-stone of an International Wolf Center, currently being planned for Ely, Minnesota, in the heart of wolf range.

The Wolf Center will also feature a captive wolf pack, wolf education programs for schoolchildren, college students and adults, lectures, videos, movies and displays, and a staging area for public field trips to hear wolves howl and to see them from aircraft.

The atmosphere that has promoted this refreshing change in attitude about wolves is the same atmosphere that has generated Candace Savage's Wolves. *This book, including some of the best wolf photos that have ever been taken by some of the world's leading wolf photographers, will surely add further to the atmosphere that helped produce it. I cannot help but think that, as its readers page through the book, more and more of them will join the ranks of the 75 per cent of people in Minnesota's wolf range who agree with the statement, "I may never see a timber wolf in the wild, but it is important for me to know they exist."*

L. David Mech

MYTHS & MONSTERS

Even as you read these words, wolves are loping through the forests and across the barrens of northern North America. Their noses to the wind, they hunt and play, feed and rest, just as their ancestors have for millions of years. There are thousands of them still, as wild as the vast lands they roam. For many people, their presence is a sign that the Earth, in special places, is still fully alive.

A few decades ago, that same knowledge would have caused a shudder of dread and, perhaps, a renewed attempt to wipe the species out—an attempt that came close to success.

The wolf, *Canis lupus,* once the most widely distributed land mammal in the world, could formerly be found throughout the northern hemisphere wherever there were large mammals for it to hunt. The species is now extinct, or nearly so, over much of its natural range. From Scandinavia to Portugal, Italy to Israel and Iran to Nepal, the story is the same: only small, scattered populations of wolves can now be found. In all of Eurasia, significant numbers remain in Greece and Spain, perhaps 4,000 animals in total, and in China and the U.S.S.R.

Nobody knows how many wolves are left. In Canada, where the species has been lost from about a fifth of its original range, there may be forty or fifty thousand. (Wolves are absent from the southern third of the country and from Newfoundland.) There are probably another five to seven thousand in Alaska. In the rest of the continent,

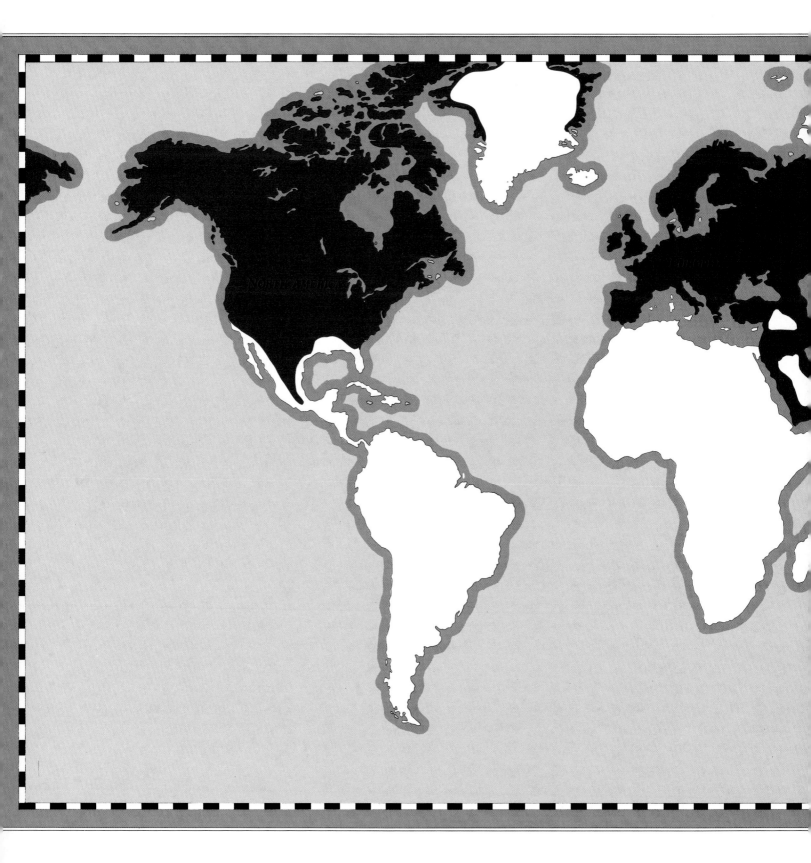

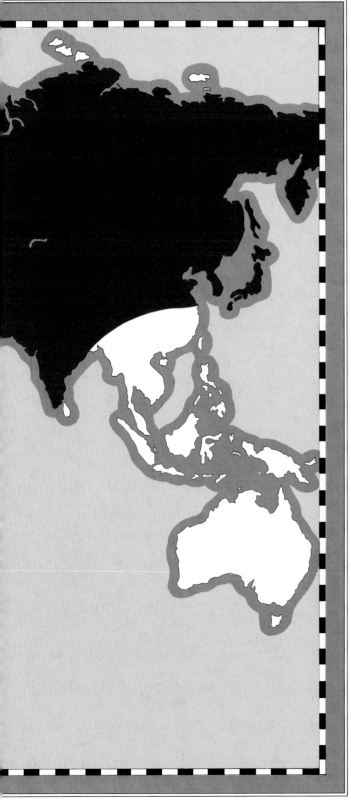

HISTORICAL GLOBAL DISTRIBUTION OF WOLVES

The wolf was once the most widely distributed land mammal in the world. This map shows its former historical range throughout Europe, Asia and North America.

Based on information provided by the Northwest Wildlife Preservation Society, Vancouver, B.C.

  PAST DISTRIBUTION OF WOLVES

estimates are easier to come by because there is little to estimate. About twelve hundred wolves live in northern Minnesota and a few (so few they have to be counted individually) can be found in nearby Wisconsin, upper Michigan, Isle Royale and Glacier national parks, Flathead National Forest, and in Idaho. In the southern half of the continent, the species is all but gone. The cause of this extinction has been human persecution, aggravated by habitat loss; and people are still the principal agents of death in most wolf populations.

For whether we are aware of it or not, our world is also inhabited by another kind of wolf, one that lives only in the wildness of the human mind. A shadowy, half-demonic beast, it peers slyly out from the dusk of semi-consciousness. For too long, this fictitious creature has succeeded in persuading us that it is the real wolf. This, by and large, is the animal we have hunted and killed.

If we hope now to live well with wolves, we must understand why, for so long, we have failed to do so or even to try. If we have been mistaken in our hatred, how did this error originate? Why have we held to our distorted views with such passionate certainty? Before we can see wolves as they are, we must first clear our minds.

It is impossible to trace the relationship between wolves and humankind to its origins, but we are entitled to surmise that it extends back at least two million years. Even then, wolves lived much as they do today, and our far-distant ancestors may have watched them running single-file through the forests, hunting hoofed animals on green grass prairies and bearing their pups in the comfort of sand dens. Indeed, our ancestors may have followed a similar lifeway themselves, travelling in small family groupings and feasting on what they could kill.

Sometimes, in ritual admiration, did these ancient hunters seek the wolf in themselves? Could this be why Neolithic artists sometimes sketched wolflike images on the walls of their caves?

One indirect way to explore these intriguing possibilities is to consider the stories and practices of native Americans. Obviously, the fact that contemporary native elders think and act in a certain way cannot tell us unequivocally what their ancestors thought and did. Nor is there any reason to believe that all ancient people have conducted themselves in the same way throughout the span of human history. Still, the traditions of native cultures bring us as close as we now can get to the world view of hunting peoples, which is ancestral to us all.

In the Canadian Museum of Civilization in Ottawa, there is a small ivory carving that was crafted long ago by a member of the Tuniit, the people who preceded the modern Inuit in the central Arctic. A simple, upright, female form, it combines a human body with the head of a wolf. What can it tell us about the possibility and desirability to a hunting people of union with wolves?

Half a continent to the south and hundreds of years afterwards, a European artist and traveller recorded a Plains Indian hunting scene. In the near distance, he depicted two white wolves stalking buffalo; in their front "paws" they clasp arrows and bows. Clearly, these are not animals but human hunters, draped in wolf skins, seeking the power and skill of their four-footed allies.

The Pawnee, aboriginal people of Kansas and Nebraska, had a language of hand signs. The signal for wolf was a U formed by the second and third finger of the right hand, held beside the right ear and then brought forward. The same sign meant Pawnee.

Inuit carving.

I am not trying to persuade you that all native ancestors sought identification with wolves; nor even that they always thought of them with reverence. Nevertheless, these themes are strong in native American cultures from tundra to rain forest, from sprucewoods to plains. The practical basis for this sympathy is not difficult to discern. In his book *Hunters on the Barrens*, anthropologist Georg Henriksen tells how the Naskapi of Labrador search for caribou.

. . . the hunters quickly shuffle away from camp. . . . [They] walk at a fast and steady pace, keeping up the same speed hour after hour. When from a hilltop the men spot caribou some miles in the distance they set off at a brisk pace. . . .

No words are spoken. Half running, every man takes the wind, weather and every feature of the terrain into account and relates it to the position of the caribou. Suddenly one of the men stops and crouches, whistling low to the other men. He has seen the herd. Without a word the men scatter in different directions. No strategy is verbalized, but each man has made up his mind about the way in which the herd can best be tackled. Seeing the other men choose their directions, he acts accordingly.

It would be hard to imagine a better description of the general hunting strategy of wolves.

The profound similarities between human and wolf have been both apparent and important to native Americans over the centuries. In some traditions, this kinship is believed to transcend even death; for in the spirit world, wolves are uniquely powerful. When they howl, is it spirit talk? According to a Cree myth, it was wolf who, after the great flood, carried a ball of moss round and round the survivors' raft, until the earth reformed. There is another story, too—a true one— about a Crow shaman named Bird Shirt, who used wolf spirit-medicine to save the warrior Swan's Head. Swan's Head had been shot through the lungs in battle. Daubed with clay to resemble a wolf and carrying his ceremonial wolf skin, Bird Shirt danced. An eyewitness reports:

Suddenly the drums changed their beating. They were softer and much faster. I heard Bird Shirt whine like a wolf mother that has young pups, and saw him trot, as a wolf trots, around the body of Swan's Head four times. Each time he shook his rattle in his right hand, and each time dipped the nose of the wolf skin in water and sprinkled it upon Swan's Head, whining continually as a wolf mother whines to make her pups do as she wishes.

I was watching—everybody near enough was watching—when Swan's Head sat up. We then saw Bird Shirt sit down like a wolf, with his back to Swan's Head, and howl four times, just as a wolf howls four times when he is in trouble and needs help.

Bird Shirt continued to dance, to trot, to circle, to whine; he made magical movements with his wolf skin—and, we are told, Swan's Head stood up, walked to the stream, stretched to release the black blood from his wounds, bathed in the water. He was healed.

Native North Americans were not the only people to seek power through ritual transformations into animals. As late as the seventh century A.D., a council of the Christian church found it necessary to denounce people who put on the heads of beasts or "make themselves into wild animals." Some scholars contend that the European belief in werewolves (literally "man-wolves") originated in just such practices. In Rome, for example, well into historic times, there were several active wolf cults. Dis Pater was the Roman version of the Lord of Death who often wore a wolf head. He was equated with the horned god Pan, whose ritual celebrations were infamous for their passionate disorder. The "wolves of Soracte" were a company of Dis Pater's priests who held ceremonies on a mountain north of Rome, dancing barefoot on burning wood and attempting to appease the gods by acting like wolves and living as predators.

Another, more famous community of wolf priests was associated with the same god, under the name of Faunus Lupercus (from *lupus,* or wolf) and with the cave of Lupercal on the northwest slope of Palatine, where Romulus and Remus, the founders of Rome, had been suckled by the She-wolf. Every year, on February 15, these priests celebrated the festival of Lupercalia. Marked with the blood of a sacrificed goat, howling with ritual laughter, they paraded naked through the city, scourging any woman that they met with sanctified goat hair to ensure her fertility. This outpouring of wolf magic was so important to the Roman state that the cult was reorganized and restored by Augustus.

Bizarre as this practice may seem, it is nonetheless worth pausing for a moment to consider its significance. The ritual invokes predation and death with the blood of the goat, sexuality with the naked dancing. And through those forces of blood and nakedness, the participants receive the promise of fertility, new life. This transformation is possible through the agency of the wolf, the killer, born in the cave-womb of the Earth, who runs, dances, howls. The wolf of Lupercalia seems to have embodied the essential principles of vitality, including death.

There are scholars who believe that the She-wolf who nurtured Romulus and Remus and thus served as foster mother to Roman civilization was the Etruscan goddess Lupa. In their view, the story represents both the historic antecedents of the city and also the mythic antecedents of the patriarchal gods.

Suggestively, the Great Goddess in her various manifestations—as Artemis, as Cerridwen—seems often to have been accompanied by wolves and dogs. Just as the deity herself was both the giver and destroyer of life, so too were her animal companions.

George Catlin, Buffalo Hunt under the Wolf-Skin Mask,
1832–1833. Oil on canvas, 24'' x 29'', 1985.66.414

Courtesy of National Museum of American Art, Smithsonian Institution

The wolves who inhabit the realm of the gods have a vivid presence; but they are nonetheless unreal. These animals have never felt the cold of an ice-covered lake against the pads of their feet, nor met one another in friendly, wag-tailed greeting. They are dream wolves, story wolves, who do what we, as dreamers and storytellers, need them to do. We human beings have a natural zest for learning and a passionate curiosity about the touch-it, taste-it, feel-it of the world around us; we are and must always have been empiricists. We are also, just as durably, myth-makers, with a compulsion for meaning and self-expression. Where meaning does not exist we create it, letting the moulding heat of our imaginations bend and transform any recalcitrant facts. Our stories and ideas become the mirrors—curving, fun-house mirrors—in which we perceive the world around us. We are not able to seize the world as it is or as it knows itself. Inevitably, our knowledge is an interaction between the reality we have created within ourselves, with all our assumptions and preconceptions, and the reality that surrounds us. We need to keep this fully in mind as we proceed.

The idea of wolf children, as encountered in the story of Romulus and Remus, seems to be an example of myth making in action. There is no doubt that it is an ancient and fecund motif. Tu Kueh—legendary founder of the Turkish nation—Zoroaster and Siegfried are all said to have been fostered by female wolves. Even in our time, the stories persist. One of the most convincing dates from 1920, near Calcutta, where an orphanage-keeper, Rev. J. A. L. Singh, claimed to have discovered two young girls (later named Amala and Kamala) in a wolf den. He found them, he said, huddled together with two wolf pups in the care of three adult wolves. The children could not walk; they preferred darkness

and raw meat; they bit and howled. Had they indeed been reared by wolves? To be sure, the story may be true; but when two scientists went to India in the 1950s to investigate, they discovered that the Reverend Singh had a disappointing reputation for untruth. A more plausible, and more tragic, explanation has been put forward by psychologist Bruno Bettelheim, who observes that the behaviour reported for Amala, Kamala and other so-called feral children coincides almost perfectly with the symptoms of severe autism, or childhood schizophrenia. If Amala and Kamala were disturbed children who had been abandoned at Singh's orphanage, might he not have allowed himself the luxury of a little lie in accounting for their plight? We know that wolves do enjoy an intimate, playful family life not unlike our own, so the notion that wolves might suckle children is at least plausible.

But if this idea is in rough harmony with the facts, it does not fit so well with the rest of European and Euro-American wolf lore as it has come down to us. Some time during the last several centuries, the wolf who seemed capable of serving as a potential protector of infants has been supplanted by a wolf in the guise of blood-thirsty fiend. Who's afraid of the big, bad wolf? Most of us are.

We have already speculated that hunting people, including our forebears, tend to view wolves with admiration and sometimes with awe. And we have also seen that in Europe, well into classical times, wolves were sometimes associated with the essential ambiguities of life and death. Then why have we been left with the slavering, grandmother-eating monster of Little Red Riding Hood? What motivated U.S. president Theodore Roosevelt to revile the wolf as "the beast of waste and desolation" and cry for its destruction? Why was it that one of the first acts passed by the Parliament of Upper Canada offered a cash payment to anyone who would rid the country of a wolf?

We are not talking here about carefully monitored wolf "control." We are talking about a hysterical hatred that, over several centuries, led to the virtual extermination of wolves from Europe, the continental United States and the settlement belt in Canada.

One source of this unbalanced passion was economic. Wolves specialize in killing large, hoofed mammals: moose, deer, muskoxen, caribou and, where they can get at them, sheep, goats and cows. It is significant that Theodore Roosevelt had a ranch on the American frontier. Wolf predation on livestock has been a problem since the beginnings of agriculture. According to a second-century Greek writer, the technique of killing troublesome wolves with poisoned meat can be traced back through antiquity to the god Apollo (curiously a wolf god himself). As soon as human beings began to tend flocks, wolves were forced into the role of enemy.

The frustration and expense of wolf predation must certainly have contributed to the wolf-as-demon mythology. So has fear, together with the curious pleasure we humans sometimes take from being scared. Wolves do attack people, though it must be emphasized from the outset that this event is extremely rare in our era. Some authorities, including wolf experts David Mech and the late Douglas Pimlott, deny that a healthy North American wolf ever poses any significant threat to a human being. Notice the caveats: they say "healthy," because rabid wolves are unequivocally dangerous; and "North American," because some people believe that European wolves may be somewhat more aggressive than those in the New World. According to Fin-

nish biologist Erkki Pulliainen, several people have been killed by wolves in Finland and the Soviet Union in recent decades; but astonishingly, the number of documented fatalities in North America stands at zero. The few confrontations that have occurred have generally ended less happily for the wolves than for their human "victims."

In ten years of radio-collaring wolves and caribou, wildlife biologists in the Northwest Territories have been attacked only twice. One of the wolves was rabid; the second was after a caribou that the biologists were working on. In both cases, the people escaped with nothing worse than nightmares.

Around Yellowknife, where I live, as around other communities in northern Canada, there are always wolves living as scavengers. The animals are extremely wary and seldom show themselves, though every now and then the children at my daughter's school are warned that a wolf has been sighted in town. Few people realize that the animals are always here and that the only "fatalities" have been dogs.

And then there are the thousands of children who camp and canoe in the wolf country of Ontario's Algonquin Park every year. How many reports have you read of children being hurt, or even frightened?

One final example, because it is so astonishing: in the mid-1950s, a researcher named D. F. Parmelee and a companion captured two small wolf pups on Ellesmere Island. They then shot several ptarmigan and headed back to camp, the pups in their arms, the birds dangling over their shoulders. Suddenly they sensed something behind them. It was the bereaved female wolf, "her nose touching the ptarmigans as they swayed back and forth." Parmelee writes, "Incredible as it surely is, we several times had to drive that wolf off with snowballs for fear that we would lose our specimens!" The wolf spent the night outside their tent, harming neither humans nor human property.

This story reveals the true nature of wolves. Their usual response to people is not aggression but curiosity or fear. What then do we make of the notorious "beasts of Gévaudan," two animals that, in the 1760s, are reported to have killed up to a hundred people, mostly small children, in south central France? How do we account for claims in a century-old scientific monograph that 161 people in Russia were killed and eaten in 1875; or reports in reputable North American newspapers that two villagers in northwest Turkey met a similar fate during a blizzard in 1968? Some of these stories do have a partial basis in fact: careful research has determined that the killers at Gévaudan were probably a small number of wolf-dog hybrids, which combined the wolf's strength and savvy with the dog's orientation towards people. Since the people of the time "knew" that wolves were monstrous, they launched an assault on the entire species. Over a period of about thirty years, two thousand wolves were killed in misplaced retribution.

It is our erroneous impression of wolves that is responsible for most reports of wolf attacks. Such stories have less to do with the biology of wild animals than with the psychology of western European Christianity over several difficult centuries. Wolves, as we have seen, speak to the human mind with the power of myth: they represent the energy of the Earth, human vitality, the mysteries of life. These include sex. It is not by accident that the Latin words for "wolf" and "whore" are identical, that in English we refer to a sexually aggressive man as a wolf, and that when a girl has her first intercourse, French speakers say "*elle a vu le loup.*" But for many centuries, Christianity was at war with human sexuality; "the world, the flesh, and the devil" had become potent dangers. So had the remnants of pagan religions with their nature cults and wolf magic.

So it is not surprising to learn that, well before the time of the Inquisition, the wolf had been equated with Satan: the wolf in Christ's fold. In the words of Barry Lopez, in his remarkable study *Of Wolves and Men,* "there was a great mystery about the wolf and a fabulous theater of images developed around him. He was the Devil, red tongued, sulfur breathed, and yellow eyed; he was the werewolf, human cannibal; he was the lust, greed, and violence that men saw in themselves." And so, of course, wolves were to be killed, painfully if possible, to rid the world of wickedness. Werewolves, too, together with witches, thousands upon thousands of them, were tortured until they confessed to shapeshifting and gory sexual crimes, and then were killed. Of what, exactly such people were victims is, as Lopez notes, "a question that hurts the human soul."

The same could be said of the slaughtered wolves.

When Europeans arrived en masse in North America, they brought with them eighteenth-century derivatives of these ideas about wolves and witchcraft. To them was added a new concomitant: a struggle for survival against the wilderness that was both literal and mythic. The settlers had arrived with a mission, to make a garden in a wild land. There was no place in this garden for predators. Wolves were killers, after all, and, in addition to any actual threat, reminded the newcomers uncomfortably of death—reminded them that they were ultimately not in control, even in this promised land.

On both continents wolves were persecuted with fury: hundreds of thousands were killed. In North America they were trapped and poisoned by ranchers, bounty hunters and professional "wolfers." They were shot from aircraft and from the ground. In the American wild West the last few survivors in each area were cast as outlaws and given bandit names: "Three Toes," "Mountain Billy" and "Custer Wolf." A hundred and fifty men tried to kill Three Toes and collect the gold watch offered in reward. It was all very exciting.

We cannot distance ourselves from this destruction by declaring that the people who committed it were evil. They were not deviants; many of the wolf killers were civil servants hired by democratically elected governments to carry out the public will. Virtually everyone was of the same mind: the country should be cleared of wolves. In 1909, the superintendent of Algonquin Park wrote a magazine article entitled "How shall we destroy the wolf?" Not "should we?"; that could be taken for granted even by an official custodian of nature—just "how?" In the early sixties, when the first careful study of wolves in the park was undertaken, it ended with a determined effort to collect the carcasses of wolves from the study area.

That was less than thirty years ago, yet today that action would be unthinkable. The change has been so sudden and so strong as to seem miraculous. The riotous and sometimes ridiculous experimentation of the sixties—love-ins, free sex and back-to-the-land—has lightened our spirits. Hiroshima, *Silent Spring* and the new science of ecology have changed our minds. Wolves, who just a few years before were burdened with all that was bestial and dangerous in nature and ourselves, suddenly have become the symbols of a born-again wilderness.

"In wildness," Thoreau told us, "is the preservation of the world." Many of us, with the fervour of those who know that their survival is in question, hope he was right.

One weakness inherent in our new enthusiasm for wolves is the potential for being swept into another round of myth making, in which the animals shine with the light of perfection and certain people are cast as demonic. Ultimately, there is not much profit in these fantasies, however satisfying they may be. We cannot spend our lives on the set of a Walt Disney film, where wolves are nice puppies that eat only mice, and every person who kills an animal is a shady character. Reality, as we currently understand it, is more interesting—and more challenging—than that.

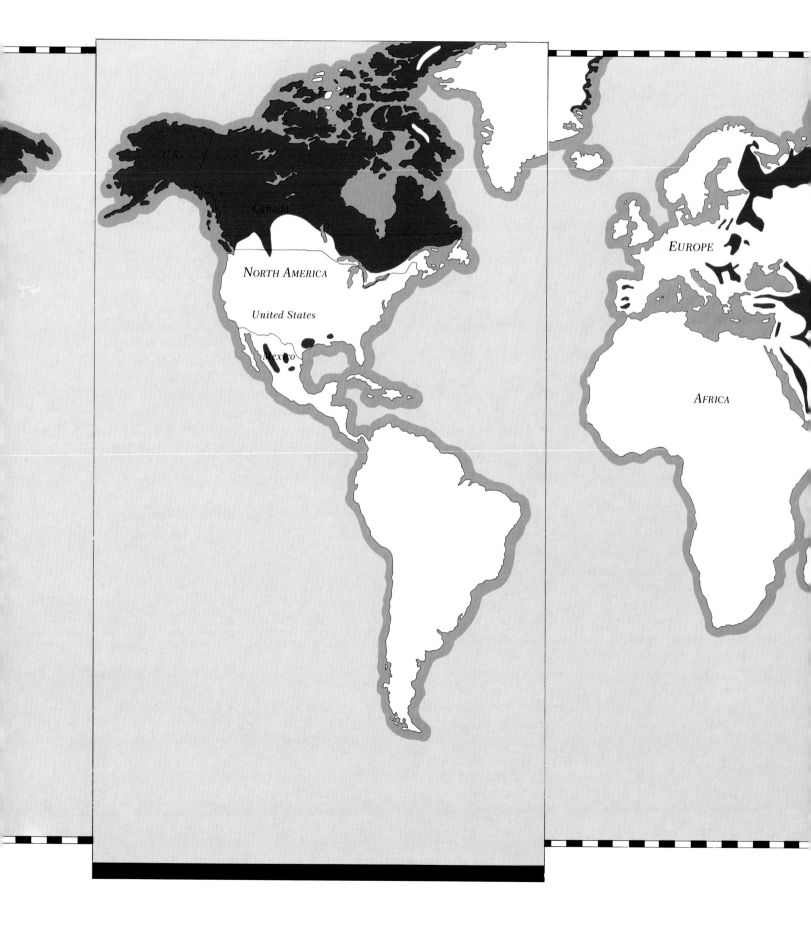

U.S.

Canada

NORTH AMERICA

United States

Mexico

EUROPE

AFRICA

PRESENT DISTRIBUTION OF WOLVES

PRESENT GLOBAL DISTRIBUTION OF WOLVES

Although the wolf has the greatest natural range of any living mammal except ourselves, it is now extinct over much of its former range. This map shows that significant numbers remain only in Greece, Spain, China and the U.S.S.R. and in northern North America (far left).

Once resident throughout the northern hemisphere, the wolf is now most at home in the wild places of northern Eurasia and North America.

Art Wolfe; inset, Stephen J. Krasemann, Valan Photos

White wolves are most common in the high Arctic.

Jim Brandenburg

Although we sometimes use terms like "timber wolves," "tundra wolves" and "grey wolves," all the wolves in the world actually belong to the same species, Canis lupus. *Grey and black animals may be born as litter mates.*

Peter J. McLeod; inset, Suzanne Henry, Prince Albert National Park

Keenly alert, a resting wolf scans its surroundings.

Jim Brandenburg

More than any other species, wolves have borne our ambiguous feelings about nature and ourselves.

Peter J. McLeod

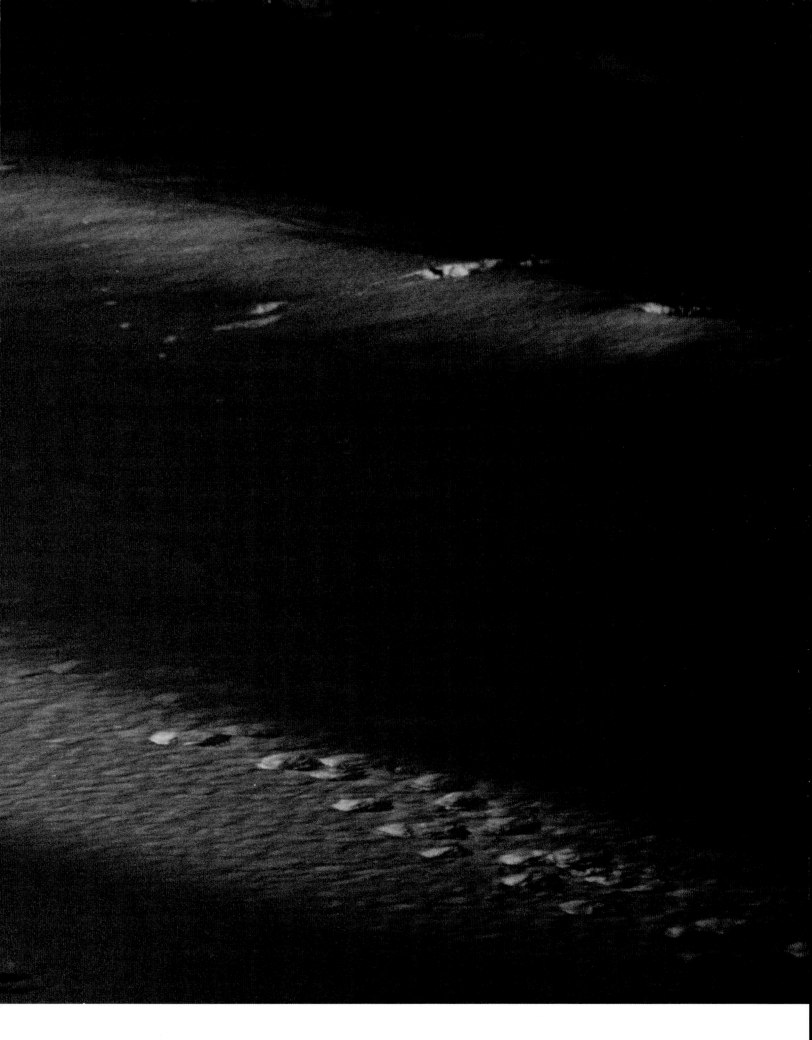

Strong and swift, wolves are the most impressive members of the wild dog family.

Jim Brandenburg

The findings of modern science remind us of what our hunting ancestors clearly knew: wolves and humans are alike in many essential ways.
Alan D. Carey

The striking Mexican wolf is virtually extinct in the wild.
Kennan Ward, DRK Photo

The red wolf of Louisiana and Texas is also within a breath
of extinction.
Tom and Pat Leeson

Two Mexican wolves engage in a ritualized tussle.

Allan Morgan, DRK Photo

Losses of livestock and game animals through predation have sometimes provided a rationale for killing wolves. But economic considerations alone cannot account for the ferocity with which the species has been persecuted in the last few hundred years.

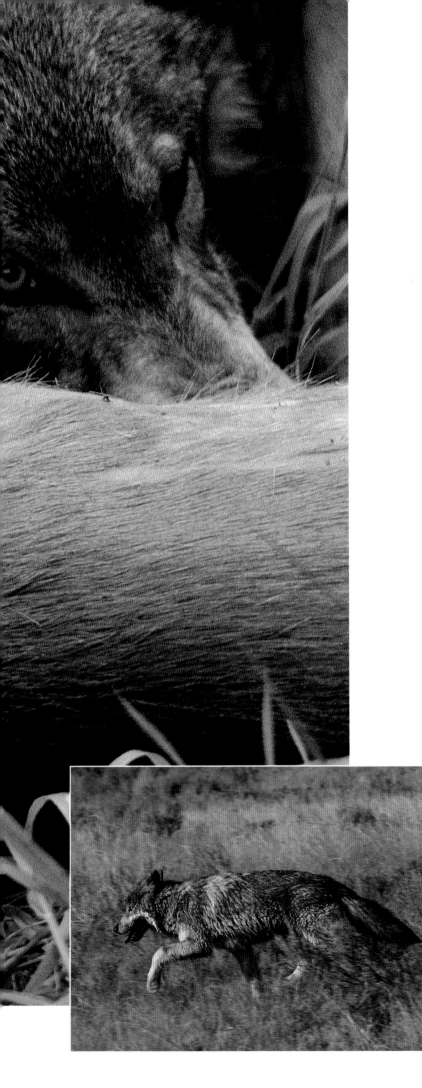

Eyes closed and muzzle raised in a characteristic howling pose, a wolf announces its presence to the world.
Karen Hollett

Through several confused and barbaric centuries, wolves have been systematically poisoned, trapped, netted, hooked, snared and shot, mainly in retribution for crimes they did not commit. The animal in the trap is more fortunate than most since it will be only temporarily detained by researchers.

Above, Fred H. Harrington; left, Harold V. Green, Valan Photos

Under natural conditions, wolves often live to be eight or nine years old, with a few individuals reaching thirteen or fourteen years. Human beings remain the principal causes of death in many wolf populations. (Above) A wolf in the prime of adulthood; inset, a bleached wolf skull.

Jim Brandenburg; inset, Art Wolfe

THE NATURE OF WOLVES

The itch of human curiosity being what it is, there are probably many things you would like to know about wolves: how big they get, how fast they run, how many pups they have, whether it's really true that they can communicate over long distances. You may be curious about their family lives, their hunting strategies and their relationship with their prey.

Surprisingly, the best place for us to begin this exploration is inside a wolf's mouth. Wolves have forty-two teeth, which fall into the same general categories as our own: incisors, canines, premolars and molars. Three special features of this arsenal call for our attention: first, the sheer number of teeth. The need to make room for them and deploy them all usefully probably accounts for the animal's characteristically long snout. Notice next the four pointed canines or "dog teeth" near the front of the jaw on bottom and top; you can see them clearly in the photograph on page 50. At lengths of up to five centimetres (two inches), these are the functional equivalent of talons and permit a wolf to pierce through tough hides and thick hair—and hang on. Imagine being able to bite through to the flesh of a woolly muskox or hook your fangs into the pendulous nose of a moose and cling there, however the animal may thrash about.

The third feature to note is the set of massive molars towards the back of the mouth, the carnassials. These specialized shearing teeth are one of the reasons that the modern line of carnivores has managed to survive. You could find them, if you dared, in the mouths of bears, weasels, mountain lions and all two hundred other members of the order Carnivora, the evolutionary line to which wolves belong.

You could also find them, at slightly less personal risk, in the mouth of a pet dog. In fact, you would find all forty-two wolf teeth there, in somewhat modified form. This is because wolves and dogs are close kin. Although the subject continues to be controversial, most authorities now agree that all dogs, from chihuahuas to dobermans, are descended from wolves which were tamed in the Near East ten or twelve thousand years ago. Others speculate that wolves were domesticated then and at several other places and times. There is no longer any serious argument in favour of another species as a major point of origin—coyote, hyena, or fox, say, or some other member of the wild dog family. It may be worth noting that in North America, coyotes, wolves and dogs all occasionally interbreed to produce both coy-wolf, coy-dog and wolf-dog hybrids, so the admixture of a little coyote blood into the dog line seems likely.

Why were wolves singled out for this intimate recognition as the first domesticated animal and "man's best friend"? To answer this question, we need to look at the ways in which wolves are different from other members of the dog family. For one thing, wolves take first place for size. Although smaller in fact than in legend, males from most areas average around 40 kilograms (95 pounds), with females about 5 kilograms (10 pounds) lighter. Measured from tip to tail, they are about as long as an adult person is tall and stand around three-quarters of a metre (two and a half feet) at the shoulder. By taming wolves, people allied themselves with this size and strength.

As hunters, early people were also able to take advantage of wolves' superior speed. More than any other carnivore, these far-ranging animals are adapted to run. For one thing, like other wild dogs, wolves enjoy a runner's leggy build. For another, through the course of evolution, they and their kin have moved up off the flat of their feet on to their toes for extra speed. But the specialization that sets wolves apart is the anatomy of their front legs which are "hung" close together, almost as if pressed into the animals' narrow chest. Their knees turn in and their paws turn outward so that the front feet swing in and set a path which the hind feet follow exactly. When they are trotting, wolves leave a neat, single line of tracks, an obvious advantage for efficient travel in deep snow or difficult country. Thanks to these physical refinements, wolves can run at 60 to 70 kilometres per hour (35 to 40 miles per hour) when pressed.

But the aspect of the wolf's nature that may have had the strongest appeal to those first would-be dog owners, as it does for us today, is the animals' ability to communicate. More than any other canid, wolves are social animals. Although some individuals live singly for periods of time (the proverbial "lone wolves"), the usual context of a wolf's life is a small family group, or pack, that includes mother and father, uncles and aunts, and siblings. Pack sizes, like most other wolf traits, vary considerably, from a single pair, which is quite common, to a community of thirty-six (recorded in Alaska), which is very rare. Most wolves live in packs of seven animals or less.

The overriding theme of wolf society is amiability. In the early 1940s, a patient, clear-headed biologist named Adolph Murie spent two summers observing a wolf den in Mount McKinley National Park, as part of the first-ever scientific study of wild wolves on this continent. What did he make of wolves' family life? "The strongest impression remaining with me after watching the wolves on numerous occasions," he wrote, "was their friendliness." This is despite all the inevitable irritations of group living: a pup who wants to jump on your head, a sibling who hogs the best sleeping place, an elder who eats more than his share, and so on.

One key to the generally even-tempered atmosphere of a wolf pack is clear communication. Like people, wolves have expressive faces. Through subtle gestures of the forehead, mouth, ears and eyes, an animal can "say" how it feels and thus permit its companions to react appropriately. For example, if a wolf is afraid or insecure, it keeps its teeth covered ("See, I would never bite you"), pulls the corners of its mouth back in a smilelike "submissive grin," narrows its eyes to slanting slits, smooths its forehead and flattens its ears against its head. A confident, threatening expression is just the reverse: bared teeth, mouth-corners forward, wrinkled muzzle, frowning forehead, and erect, forward-pointing ears. Does it strike you that our own expressions are very similar? Try making an ingratiating face, as if you wanted to ease your way out of a confrontation with a bully; then scowl as if you were ready to bite off someone's head. Chances are, you won't be able to say much with your ears, but otherwise your expressions will probably resemble those of a wolf.

It is much easier for a human being to intuit the mood of a wolf or dog than that of a hamster, say, or a canary. As photographer Jim Brandenburg put it after a summer spent watching wolves in the high Arctic, "I've never seen animals that have so many characteristics that can be felt." No wonder early people chose wolves for companions.

If the first dog was pure wolf, modern dogs are so distinct from their ancestors that they are considered by many scientists to be a separate species. *Canis lupus* has become *Canis familiaris*. In addition to the obvious differences that have been artificially bred into certain lines—a dachshund or a sheepdog, for example—other more subtle changes have taken place. Even the most wolflike dogs tend to have smaller teeth, shorter muzzles and broader foreheads than wolves, making them look a little more like their human masters. They are also generally less intelligent than their wild cousins, a common result of domestication. (It would be interesting to know if the rule holds for people, too.) Dogs breed twice a year rather than once, have no scent-marking gland on the tail and have distinctively shaped skulls. To human eyes, their feet seem to be "the right size," rather than "too big" like those of their snowshoed, wild relatives. But the most significant difference is in their social attitude: dogs want to be with people, wolves want to be with wolves. According to David Mech, the bonds amongst members of a wolf pack are probably comparable to those between a dog and its human family.

In particular, Mech suggests that the relationship between Fido and his master resembles that between a low-ranking wolf and the top wolf in the pack. Wolf packs are hierarchical. A large, well-established pack may consist of a small "upper class" that includes only a single breeding pair (the "alpha" male and female); a "middle class" of non-breeding adults, each with its own individual ranking; a "lower class" of outcasts; and an up-and-coming group of immature animals, those under two years of age.

The leaders of the pack, usually the parents of the younger animals, wear their status with confidence: in social encounters, they stand tall, hold their ears and tails erect, and freely look other animals directly in the eye. Simply by doing this they are declaring and reinforcing their superior rank. A subordinate animal, on the other hand, cringes towards the leader on bent legs, tail low and ears slicked back. Like a pup begging food, it bunts its nose against the superior's face in greeting, as if to say "I'm little and you're big; I like you, so please be nice to me." This gesture has been dubbed "active submission." If the subordinate animal feels a need to make its point more forcefully—"I accept that you are the leader and that I am a social underling; I'm no threat to you"—it may sprawl on its back with its feet in the air, like a dog that wants its belly scratched. This behaviour, known as "passive submission," may also carry a reference to infancy, because it is very like the position of a tiny pup that is being massaged by an adult to make its bowels work. You can look for these dominance/submission routines in the wolf cage at the zoo, or see how the wolves react if you use your hands to mimic ears-up and ears-back postures. (Ironic though it may seem, most of our intimate knowledge of these spirits of the wilderness has been gained by observing animals in captivity.)

If luck is on your side, you may also have a chance to watch a wolf "greeting ceremony," one of those joyful, wagful, face-licking get-togethers when the animals rediscover one another after waking from a snooze or reunite after a brief separation. In the wild, these celebrations of family solidarity also often occur when the animals first scent game before a hunt, or after a kill. Frequently, the focus of the festivities is the leading male, who suddenly

finds himself closely surrounded by half a dozen eager, howling subordinates, who all try to plaster up beside him and stick their muzzles in his face. This is, in fact, a group demonstration of "active submission," a declaration of joint affinity for the dominant animal. Through this ritual, the animals define their group—"this is us; all other wolves are outsiders"—and reaffirm the status of the alpha male.

It may surprise you to learn that the dominant male is generally not particularly aggressive, at least not towards other members of his pack. In fact, quite the opposite is likely to be true—most top-ranking males are exceptionally tolerant and friendly. Wolves in a pack are constantly checking one another, with a sniff to the coat here, a lick on the cheek there; and no animal is more active in seeking and receiving this kind of routine social contact than the dominant male. Together with the other top-ranking animals, but even more than they, he provides an emotional centre for the community. As the constant recipient of gestures of active submission, he is a focus of friendly feeling in the pack. One of his most important social functions, then, is to help maintain the even temper and cohesiveness of the group. If he loses his high position to another wolf (and such coups are accomplished from time to time), he may also lose his ability to serve the pack in this way. The function generally belongs to the office of top wolf, not to the individual who happens to hold that rank.

Another important responsibility of many alpha males is maintaining the pack's hunting territory. As a Russian proverb observes, "The wolf is kept fed by his feet." But that does not mean that the animals travel aimlessly across the countryside. Instead, most packs restrict their journeys to the familiar trails and crossroads of a large tract of land. Just how large depends on the size of the pack and the density of game that is available. On northeastern Vancouver Island, British Columbia, for example, where black-tailed deer are abundant, a pack of ten wolves occupied an area of around 60 square kilometres (25 square miles). In Michigan, by contrast, where game is less plentiful, a group of four required 650 square kilometres (260 square miles) and in Alberta, a pack of eight ranged over more than 1300 square kilometres (540 square miles). Just as a statistically average person, with its 1.6 mates and 2.4 offspring, is an improbable fiction, so is a numerically average wolf territory. Averages don't exist in nature, especially not in the nature of wolves. As we have seen, a wolf territory might conceivably be as small as 50 or as large as 1500 square kilometres (20 to 600 square miles)—a thirty-fold variability. This extraordinary capacity to adapt their behaviour to local conditions is one of the reasons that wolves were formerly so widespread.

Whatever the size of the territory, that area is the pack's home ground and exclusive domain. The resident animals do not willingly share their land with other wolves, and intruders can expect a rough reception, especially from the dominant male. Adolph Murie tells of a spring morning in Alaska when he was watching a pack of wolves laze around their den. But the leading male seemed uneasy and moved to a lookout position just above the others. What was upsetting him? "Shortly after noon the four wolves at the den joined [him] and they all bunched up, wagging tails and expressing much friendliness." That was when Murie noticed a sixth wolf, "a small gray animal, about 50 yards from the others. All the [resident] wolves trotted to the stranger and practically surrounded it, and for a few moments I thought that they would be friendly toward it

for there was just the suggestion of tail wagging by some of them. But something tipped the scales the other way for the wolves began to bite at the stranger. It rolled over on its back, begging quarter. The attack continued, however, so it scrambled to its feet and with difficulty emerged from the snapping wolves. Twice it was knocked over as it ran down the slope with the five wolves in hot pursuit."

The four subordinate wolves soon quit the chase, but the leading male went on, giving the intruder no option but escape. Says Murie, "The unfortunate stranger's hip and base of tail were soaked with blood. It was completely discouraged in its attempt to join the group, for it was not seen again." Had it persisted, it might have been killed.

For the most part, wolves avoid this kind of bloodshed by keeping out of foreign territories. How can they tell where they've crossed onto occupied land? Wolf territories are all thoroughly posted with No Trespassing signs in the form of "scent posts." These are simply conspicuous objects—stumps, logs, rocks, chunks of ice, and so on—along trails, at crossroads and, especially, near the edges of the territory, which the wolves mark by urinating on them. This medium of communication may not be very elegant by human standards, but it works. Most of the marking is done by the dominant animals, primarily the alpha male, who doles his urine out in dribbles every quarter kilometre or so. (This explains why it can take so long to walk the dog!) Sometimes a whole line of wolves will wait patiently for a turn to leave their mark on a scent post. Perhaps this is another way of demonstrating group solidarity for, as researcher Russ Rothman once observed, "Wolves that pee together stay together."

Wolves have an extraordinary sense of smell—in the right wind, they can detect moose at two kilometres (a mile and a half)—and probably obtain a great deal of information from their scent marks. They may even use them in finding their way around. Through experience, wolves are believed to develop mental maps of their territories on which locations such as kill sites and trail junctions are registered. Thus, it is probably significant that the crossroads of trails—the decision points for efficient route-finding—are generously scent-marked, making them vivid and memorable.

Because our own sense of smell is weak, we are at a loss to properly decode these olfactory messages, but it seems possible that wolves pick up more personal information as well: which individuals were last here, which sex they are, who is travelling together, and how long it was since the area was hunted. At the very least, it is clear that they can distinguish between fresh marks and old ones, and can tell when they pick up a stranger's scent. This latter conclusion is based on the fact that the animals scent-mark much more frequently near the borders than in the core of their territories—and it is usually at the borders that they can detect the scent of neighbouring packs. (There is often a narrow band of overlap, about a kilometre wide, which the two packs use at different times.) The foreign odours apparently stimulate the animals to leave their mark on the disputed zone—and then to turn right around and head for the safety of their own territory.

Assuming that they are relatively well fed, wolves would even rather lose a meal than trespass on another pack's land. Biologists working in northeastern Minnesota tell the story of a pack that had chased and wounded a deer. The prey was badly hurt, yet on it ran, with the wolves on its heels. But when it crossed a river that served as the dividing line between two territories, the wolves followed for a short distance, then stopped, scent-marked and trotted back home. The next day, the neighbouring pack killed and ate the deer.

Another way in which wolves lay claim to their territory is with sound. Wolves are chatty creatures: in close-up communication, they use a variety of noises—whimpers, whines, squeaks, yelps, barks, snarls and growls—to amplify and clarify the meaning of their facial and body gestures. Laboratory analysis suggests that slight differences in these vocalizations may signal subtle differences in the message. For example, a whimper always indicates a friendly, non-aggressive attitude, but a special chirplike tone expresses sexual interest, a longish squeak indicates an intention to howl, a sharp whine may put an end to an interaction with another wolf, and so on. Exactly how detailed this language is, we may never know, because an oscilloscope is, at best, a clumsy substitute for the wolf's finely tuned ears.

For long-distance communication, wolves raise their voices in that most evocative of all wolf sounds, their cool, lingering howl. The power of this song for human hearers is mystifying. Why should these rising harmonies, uttered by another species for communication with its own kind, echo so strongly through the human mind? Why do they speak to us of wildness and make us quiver with wonder or with dread? In recent years, thousands of people have had a chance to experience these sensations at first hand by participating in "wolf howls." Picture a long line of cars creeping through the dusk of a wilderness park, then rolling to a stop. The occupants quietly get out, turn their faces to the sky—and howl, then listen. Sometimes, about one time in ten, the human howlers are rewarded by a response; for just as people respond psychically to wolves, so wolves often answer people directly. This fact has been used by wildlife biologists to get an idea of wolf densities in particular areas, notably in Algonquin Park: the more frequently the biologists get a response, the greater the number of wolves are presumed to be present.

Interestingly, this technique does not work nearly so well if the human howls are recorded instead of live. Wolves are much less likely to answer recordings. Although human ears cannot distinguish between the two sources, tests reveal very slight distortions on the tape. If the wolves can detect these minor anomalies, imagine what they might be able to discern in natural howls. Just as each person has a unique singing voice, so individual wolves have distinct howls. For example, a particular wolf may always begin and end in a certain way, stay within a certain range of pitches, or include a specific jump from pitch to pitch. Can wolves recognize one another at a distance by these characteristics? Does a howl reveal what the animal is doing or how it is feeling? It has been proven that a wolf which is walking slowly howls slightly differently than if it were lying down or pacing, and one that is sending out an unsolicited message sings higher than if it were responding to another animal. Some people think the howling of a wolf that is isolated from its companions broadcasts a particularly plaintive, lonesome-sounding complaint. Whether or not wolves can send messages such as "the hunting over here is pretty bad and I am going to stay another week," as Farley Mowat would have us believe, definitely remains to be seen!

As nearly as we can tell, wolves often howl simply because they love to. A group howl (the "greeting ceremony" described earlier) has been likened to a community singsong. According to Lois Crisler, who kept free-ranging wolves in Alaska for several years, some animals "will run from any distance, panting and bright-eyed, to join in, uttering, as they near, fervent little wows, jaws wide, hardly able to wait to sing." Each animal joins in at its own pitch, for, as Crisler observed, "wolves avoid unison singing; they like chords." A typical howling bout lasts just over a minute, with a pause of at least twenty minutes between bouts. By participating in these festivities, wolves probably strengthen the amicable feeling between themselves and other members of the pack.

Howling can also serve to reunite the pack physically, if members have separated to hunt alone or in small groups. Wolves have an uncanny ability to pinpoint the source of a howl and use it to locate their companions. In open terrain, a mere human can hear howls 16 kilometres (10 miles) away and, if the sound is muffled by woods, at half that distance. A wolf's hearing is, of course, more far-reaching than our own.

In addition to providing long-distance communication amongst pack members, howls also serve as a means of contact between packs. On a calm night, a single howling bout can advertise a pack's presence over an area of up to 300 square kilometres (120 square miles). Many researchers think that howling is a means of territorial defence among wolves, just as singing is among many species of birds. "This land is our land," the wolf pack cries; and the neighbouring pack may reply, "And this is ours." Sometimes as many as three packs will chorus back and forth, each within its own territory; then each will retreat from its neighbours.

By now, you may have concluded that the defence of territories—laying exclusive claim to familiar den sites, resting places, travel routes and food resources—is an essential characteristic of wolves. And so it is, with one important and quite amazing exception. Wolves that live on the tundra do not adhere to this seemingly basic pattern. Although they associate in packs for much of the year, they are not territorial because they cannot afford to be. Their primary prey, the barren-ground caribou, undergoes a dramatic annual cycle of migrations, sweeping south to the forests for winter, north to the tundra to calve, taking a certain route one year, dodging a hundred kilometres to east or west the next, defying all prediction by either human or wolf. Except for spring and early summer when they are denning, tundra wolves are also migratory, trailing the herds up and down the northern third of the continent. What role scent-marking and howling might play for these animals, or even how they organize and maintain their packs, is not yet understood.

One hint that a different social system may operate among tundra wolves than elsewhere is the high percentage of northern females that become pregnant every year. This is not at all the case in territorial packs where, typically, only one female and one male—usually the highest ranking animals—breed in a given season. Sometimes this happens because the alpha pair are the only sexually mature animals in the pack, the others being youngsters less than two years old. But even in packs that have several adults of each sex, the general rule is that only the "top dogs" will breed. Fully 94 per cent of the wolf packs that have been studied produced only one litter per year.

This remarkably effective birth control is achieved through social interaction. Strictly speaking, the breeding season lasts for about four weeks in late winter, sometime between January and April depending on latitude. It is during this period that the adult females come into oestrus, or "heat," and are able to reproduce. But preparations for mating begin much earlier, often in the fall, and are marked by a sudden increase in social tension: snarling, snapping, fights. The ringleader in this outburst of aggression, the one who initiates most of the attacks, is the dominant bitch; her animosity is directed towards the other female adults. Under assault by the entire pack, these animals become temporary outcasts, who often live alone, on the fringes of group activity.

As you might expect, when the actual mating time comes, it is the dominant female and not one of her oppressed subordinates who initiates courtship. She does this by making gestures of intense submission towards the high-ranking males and by squirting urine on bushes, trees, rocks and other places where it is likely to be noticed. At first the males don't seem to know what is going on, but after a while they catch the excitement of the season and start crowding around her, touching her muzzle, snuffling her body, sniffing her ambrosial pee, peeing on her ambrosial pee—ah, bliss. Soon, all the males in the pack, even the pups, will be following in her wake.

They will not, however, all have a chance to breed. In part, the choice is made by the female, who likes some of the males and rejects others. But she is really not terribly choosey and is quite willing to let herself be seduced. Eventually, her independence is curtailed by one of the top-ranking males (usually the alpha male) who takes charge and attempts to prevent other males from mating. So we now have a situation in which the top-ranking female (at this moment, the most aggressive animal in the pack) is continuing to suppress her same-sex rivals, and the top-ranking male has begun to do the same. The only opportunity that subordinate animals have to mate is when the dominant pair is busy. One young male got his chance when the alpha male was feeding; a second pair was able to breed when the chief animals were literally "tied up." (Like dogs, mating wolves remain physically attached to each other for about fifteen minutes in a copulatory tie.)

It has often been said that wolves mate for life, and it does seem to be true that breeding animals tend to breed with the same partners in successive years. But this is obviously not the result of a hearts-and-flowers, till-death-do-us-part loyalty. To be sure, wolves do have personal relationships and form strong bonds with one another, but these preferences are not exclusive. Besides, they can only be expressed sexually if the social order permits. In one captive pack, for example, the alpha female wanted to mate with the alpha male, but he preferred the third-ranked bitch. The female then accepted the second-ranked, or beta, male, though the alpha male tried to stop this mating. Both alpha animals snarled and bit at the beta male while he was copulating with the alpha female. The next year, the alpha male was gone, so the female again accepted the beta male and two other mates. The males were interested in other females, and other females wanted to breed, but the alpha female prevented these matings by interfering.

The alpha female died the next year as the result of leg wounds inflicted by the most repressed female. Had she survived this injury, she might well have become a pack outcast, a common fate for deposed alphas. She would then have left the group or become its most submissive, hangdog member, while her successor acquired the social power and sexual privilege of high office. Had she left the pack, she might have wandered widely until she met a lone male and joined with him to initiate a new family.

(If the social structure is disrupted by the death of key individuals, the pack's social system breaks down, and contraception cannot be imposed. Where wolves are hunted or otherwise persecuted by people, for example, a high percentage of females is likely to breed. Even in the Northwest Territories, where the small human population raises the possibility that the wolves might live in relative peace, biologists are beginning to suspect that it is human harassment and not a unique social pattern that leads to the animals' unusual fecundity.)

When the females' period of oestrus ends, the agitated atmosphere of the breeding season gradually fades. If subordinate females have been suppressed, they are now readmitted to the fellowship of the pack and may even help the alpha female prepare her den. This may involve simply cleaning out a burrow that has been used in previous years, since some dens are occupied for decades; or the task may be to enlarge and renovate an old fox burrow or an abandoned beaver lodge. Alternatively, the female may decide to excavate a new hole, generally choosing a sandy hillside that promises easy digging through the still-frozen ground and good springtime drainage. She also gives preference to sites that are near a supply of drinking water, from a spring, river or lake. Work on the den or dens (for the female may prepare several) often begins about six weeks after she conceives and three weeks before the pups are born. The gestation period for wolves is about sixty-three days.

What is it like inside a wolf den? Adolph Murie decided to find out. "I wriggled into the burrow which was 16 inches high and 25 inches wide.

Six feet from the entrance of the burrow there was a right angle turn. At the turn there was a hollow, rounded and worn, which obviously was a bed much used by an adult. . . . From the turn the burrow slanted slightly upward for 6 feet" to a chamber for the pups.

It is to these snug surroundings that the female retires, alone, to give birth. As each tiny infant appears, the mother licks it hard to remove the amniotic sack, chews through the umbilical cord, then licks the baby again until it is clean, dry and snuggled against her side. It takes her about three hours to whelp a typical litter of five or six pups.

At birth, the pups can do little but squirm and suck; their awareness scarcely extends beyond warmth and warm milk. But after a couple of weeks, their eyes begin to work, dimly at first, and by three weeks they can walk, chew, growl and hear. It is at about this time that they first poke their round little heads out of the den: then let the fun begin!

Everyone who has played with a puppy dog knows how delightfully silly and full of life they are. A wolf pup is just the same, and five or six of them, growing up together in the fresh spring air, form an exuberant company. "Catch me if you can." "Don't look now! I'm going to pounce on you." "Watch me kill this old piece of caribou hide!" "I can beat up on you." All these puppy games have their serious side, since the youngsters are practising hunting skills, learning the subtleties of wolf body language and beginning to explore a variety of social relationships. But the pups are not aware of all this. They are simply rollicking with energy and the new-found enjoyment of one another's company. No matter how old they get, they will not lose these qualities; a wolf is never too old to play.

Throughout the summer, the den provides a hub for the pack's activities. Each evening, the grown-ups go off to hunt, sometimes all together, sometimes alone or in small groups. Often the mother, or a substitute babysitter, remains at the den. By mid-morning, the hunters have returned, ready to spend a long dozeful day; but before settling down to rest, each new arrival will likely be set upon by an eager mob of pups, who bite, lick and nudge insistently at the adult's mouth. This is their way of begging for food and it may stimulate the grown-up to regurgitate a heap of half-digested meat. While the pups gobble up their feast, the adults can enjoy a few moments of peace. It must be hard to sleep with a pup nibbling on your ears or using your back for a tumbling mat.

Biologists are intrigued by the involvement of subordinate pack members as "helpers" in the care of the pups. According to evolutionary theory, the sole objective of an organism's life is to be the parent, and grandparent, and great-great-grandparent of as many individuals as possible. In this way, an individual ensures that its own personal genetic material is well represented in the future stock of the species. In the "struggle for survival," this is what counts: survival of your genes into succeeding generations where they can continue to influence the course of evolution. So why would a wolf that had not been able to produce its own offspring assist in rearing another wolf's pups?

Two possible answers have been suggested. Some biologists believe that many of the so-called "helpers" are actually dependents. Perhaps they are inexperienced hunters who hang around the den so that they can follow more expert animals to their kills. Perhaps they rely on the opportunity to occasionally beg food from other members of the pack, as sometimes occurs. Do the "helpers" actually take more than they contribute? This question has not been clearly answered.

But let us assume that appearances hold, and it turns out that the "helpers" really help. An explanation for their behaviour can be sought in genetics. As we have seen, a wolf pack is a family, mostly the offspring of a single pair; it is therefore likely that the new pups and the "helpers" are brothers and sisters, or at least half-siblings. From a genetic point of view, an individual has exactly the same degree of relationship to a sibling as to its own offspring. Your daughter, for example, would carry half your genes, as would your sister. So a wolf that helps care for its younger siblings is, in fact, helping to ensure the survival of its own genes. Similarly, in cases of "communal denning"—a rare occurrence in which a subordinate female bears young and then brings them to the alpha's den to spend their infancy—both females have a genetic stake in the other's progeny.

While we have been busy with these theoretical ponderings, our litter of pups has rapidly been growing up. Sometime in the first couple of months, the mother may move her offspring to another burrow, carrying each gently in her powerful jaws. Then, when they are about eight or ten weeks old, too big and rambunctious to require a den any more, the family relocates to an open-air home, or "rendezvous site." This is an area of about a thousand square metres (half an acre) where the youngsters play and to which the adults return each day. These sites continue to be used till about September, just about the time for a new year's cycle of breeding and birth to begin.

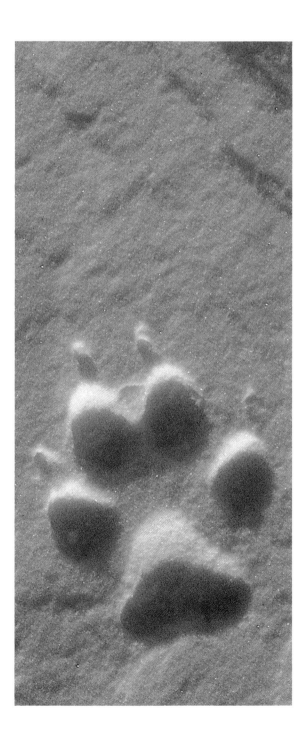

On crisp, wind-driven snow, a wolf has left its track.
Art Wolfe

Wolves inhabit a secret world, to which people can gain at best partial entrance.

Art Wolfe

Just as dogs mark their favourite light poles and fire hydrants, wolves use urine to mark their trails, kills and territorial boundaries. Often, a high-ranking male will make a "scrape" with his feet beside a urine mark, adding a visible sign to the olfactory message.

Above, Dennis W. Schmidt, Valan Photos

We are excluded from the experience of wolves by the deficiencies of our senses. Wolves, like many other animals, inhabit a rich, three-dimensional world of scents that we cannot even detect.

Left, Wayne Lankinen, Valan Photos

Wolves use their noses to find cached food. In the spring, they often bury chunks of meat near the den site, where it can be recovered and eaten by the denning female while she is confined with her young. (Inset) Nobody knows why wolves like to roll in smelly messes. Are they picking up olfactory information that will be decoded by other members of their group, or do they just like rotten-meat perfume?

Erwin and Peggy Bauer

The wolf above is scent-marking by rubbing against a carcass.

Peter J. McLeod

Although wolves may howl alone, at any season and at any time of the day, they do most of their singing in groups during winter and at dawn and dusk. This pack is assembling for a "greeting ceremony," an expression of group solidarity.

Jim Brandenburg

One reason that wolves get along so well is that they communicate clearly. Minor disputes, like the one shown above, are usually settled quickly and without a fight. The animal on the left is flattening its ears in an expression of submission and fear, while the one on the right dominates the situation with an aggressive snarl.

Peter J. McLeod

Wolves, like people, are intensely sociable. Except for the occasional "lone wolf," they generally live in groups of around half a dozen animals, mostly close relatives. Many human observers have been impressed by the friendly tone of life in a wolf pack.

Layne Kennedy

"Muzzle biting" is one of a number of ways in which wolves affirm their social relationships and maintain the peaceful, nonaggressive atmosphere of the pack.
Scot Stewart

Dark markings around the wolf's ears, eyes and muzzle accentuate its facial expressions and facilitate clear communication.
Scot Stewart

(Inset) Wolves have a variety of subtle, and not so subtle, ways of expressing hostility. Yes, they really do stick out their tongues!
Karen Hollett

"I said it—and I meant it." Minor tussles usually proceed from threat to body contact. In serious fights, which occur only rarely, physical combat begins without the social niceties of threats and warnings.

Peter J. McLeod

A momentary mealtime flare-up. The animal on the right is signalling its mixed emotions: the gaped mouth indicates aggression, but the flattened ears suggest fear.

Fred H. Harrington

(Inset) A subordinate male flees from a dominant's determined attack. This dispute, like most others in the pack, will probably be settled without bloodshed.

Peter J. McLeod

If neither contestant is intimidated by the other's threats, disputes may escalate to attacks. Above, an animal lunges at a dodging rival.

Karen Hollett

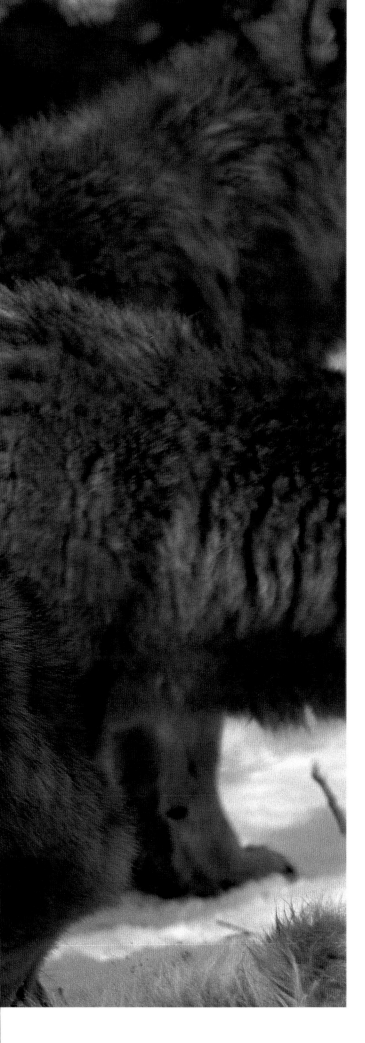

Wolves are powerful, well armed and capable of killing each other, yet serious wounds or fatalities seldom occur.
Layne Kennedy

Wolf packs have a well-established "pecking order," so that each animal knows whom it can boss and to whom it must submit. This understanding helps wolves avoid serious fights over trivial disagreements. The peaceable gesture shown here also serves as an expression of dominance.
Rolf O. Peterson

(Inset) Wolf quarrels are soon forgotten. Combatants may even lick one another's wounds. Note the scar above the eye of the wolf on the right.
Peter J. McLeod

(Inset) This animal wears the marks of a dispute with another male.

Peter J. McLeod

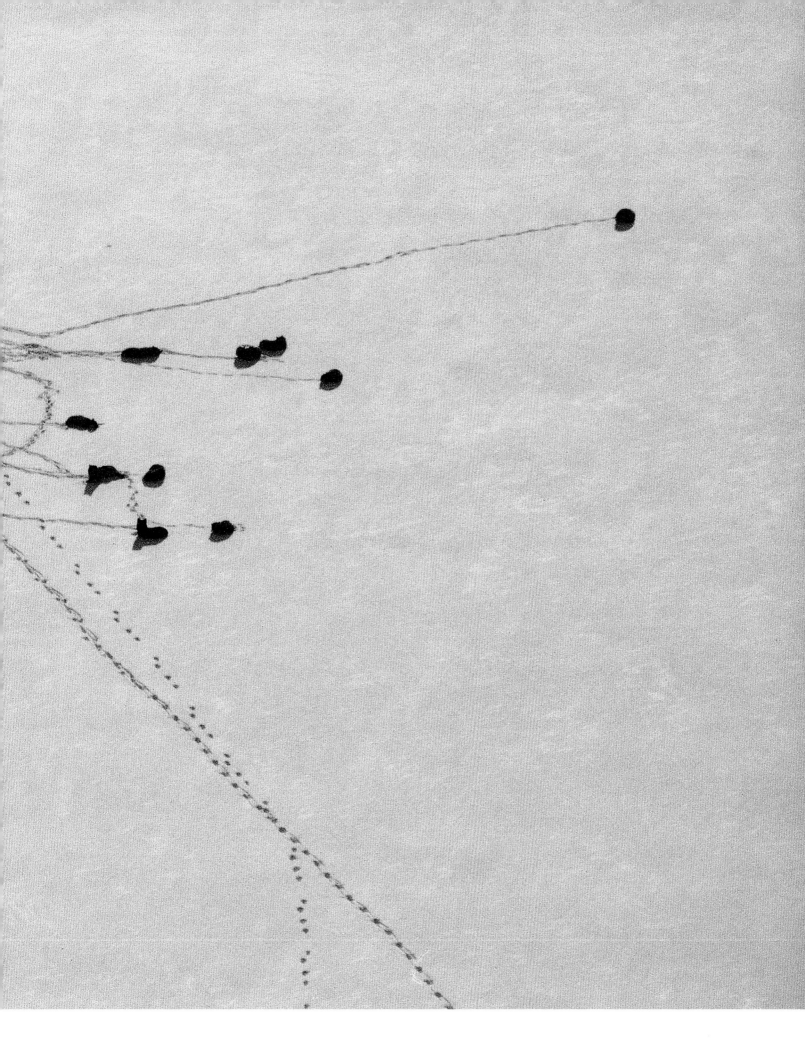

A pack may single out an individual "scapegoat" for special abuse. The wolf on the left above has just been attacked and ostracized by its companions.

Rolf O. Peterson

The most aggressive animals are the top-ranking male and
female, each of whom systematically oppresses subordinates
of the same sex. Their goal is to prevent other animals from
mating and bearing young. (Inset) Drawn to the irresistible
lure of the breeding female's urine, two males watch and
sniff attentively.

Peter J. McLeod

(Inset) A male paws at a not entirely appreciative female.
Peter J. McLeod

The female, in the lead, is followed by her consort of males.
Karen Hollett

A breeding female signals her displeasure at the attentions of a male.
Peter J. McLeod

Even in the act of mating the scrapping continues! Here, two males quarrel over a female's back as a third looks on.

Peter J. McLeod

Young wolf pups enjoy the warmth of one another's company inside their burrow.

Art Wolfe

Wolves usually den in snug, hillside digs like the one on the left.

Esther Schmidt, Valan Photos

(Inset) Heavy with pups, this breeding female will limit her activities to the vicinity of her den. The gestation period for wolves is about nine weeks.

Tom W. Hall

When the pups first emerge from the den, they remain under the watchful care of their mother or another adult. They will stay around their burrow for eight to ten weeks.

Jim Brandenburg

The infant on the right, though only two or three weeks old, is already attracted by the taste of meat.

Fred H. Harrington

(Inset) At two and a half weeks, a wolf pup struggles to the mouth of the den and raises its voice in an infant howl.

Scot Stewart

A wolf overlooks its den site on Ellesmere Island.

Jim Brandenburg

At the age of two or three weeks, these wolf pups are ready to start venturing out of the den.

Above, Scot Stewart; left, Fred H. Harrington

Gradually, through the seasons of their first year, young wolves begin to attain the appearance, if not always the dignity, of adulthood. Here, wolf pups at a rendezvous site call their companions.

Art Wolfe

These two-month-old pups display the eager alertness that is typical of their species.

Peter J. McLeod

In youthful games and interactions, wolves develop strength and skills and explore a variety of social relationships.

Peter J. McLeod

This casual grouping may be a demonstration of dominance by the animal that is standing. These pups are nine months old.

Peter J. McLeod

O N   T H E   H U N T

The first spring and summer of a young wolf's life pass in frolic and dependency, but with fall comes a crucial initiation into adulthood, as the pups join in the hunt. Hunting large ungulates, armed with nothing but one's teeth and sharp wits, is a dangerous occupation; there is much for the youngsters to learn. The first stage in their apprenticeship has been pouncing on mice and bugs back at the den and rendezvous site; the second stage will be watching the adults.

In his new book, *The Muskoxen of Polar Bear Pass,* David R. Gray tells of a wintery September day when he and a group of colleagues watched six wolves, including two pups, trot towards a herd of twelve muskoxen—towards massive, swinging horns and heavy, slashing front hooves, backed by an average body weight of more than 300 kilograms (700 pounds). "Travelling in single file, the wolves approached to within about a hundred metres of the herd, which grouped, then separated. As it shifted around, one wolf lay down as two others circled the milling herd." The herd started to run, but the dominant bull, the leader of the muskoxen, stood and faced the attackers. A wolf leaped at his flank, and the rest of the herd closed in again.

The other wolves then joined the first two and the muskoxen grouped together in a rough circle facing them. The two pups stood together watching as several adults ran around the herd. Two muskoxen charged out at one wolf, which just ran out far enough to avoid them and then moved right back to the herd again.

At this point the two pups headed away from the closely grouped herd, their tails between their legs. A bull and cow each charged as a wolf ran around the herd. Each time a muskox charged one wolf, another wolf rushed between the individual and the herd, but failed to cut off the muskox because the rest of the herd closed the gap. Four minutes after the start of the attack, the wolves left the herd and headed towards the pups. The herd remained grouped tightly together as all the wolves lay down.

In many ways, this incident is representative of wolves' general hunting behaviour. One notices, for example, the single-file travel and the collective—though by no means rigidly disciplined—assault. Here, each wolf took advantage of opportunities created by another's attack, as they attempted to isolate a muskox from the protection of the herd. There are many interesting variations on this theme of co-operation. For example, one wolf may act as a decoy, by attacking and dashing around, while the rest of the pack moves in unnoticed to take the prey by surprise. Or sometimes one or two wolves run beyond their quarry and take up positions at a distance, out of sight. When the rest of the pack chase the prey, this advance guard is waiting in ambush.

Are these co-ordinated manoeuvres the result of formal planning? Almost certainly not. It seems more likely that they are a sign of the animals' alertness and intelligence. Each individual makes its own decision about what to do, choosing from amongst its innate and learned hunting behaviours. What is the lay of the land? How is the prey responding? What actions have the other wolves begun to take? Quick—the decision is made. How do wolves consider these questions without language? We cannot know.

Obviously, a hunt requires focus, concentration, commitment. Yet it is not uncommon for wolves to break off for a short period of observation or rest ("one wolf lay down as two others circled the milling herd"), or to give up the attempt altogether even when it seems to a human observer that the predators still have a chance of success. Were Gray's wolves not hungry enough to press the attack (they did have a carcass nearby), or could they sense that it would be a waste of energy to proceed? Just because wolves want to kill an animal does not mean they will be able to. After all, they and their prey have evolved together and in response to one another for countless generations. With every increase in the wolves' hunting prowess, there has come a corresponding increase in their prey's ability to avoid predation.

It is an even match. Muskoxen, as we have seen, have the advantage of their circular defence formation, rumps in the centre, heads towards the attacker, so that their flanks are protected and their weapons deployed. Caribou are protected by their erratic migrations, which make them hard to find, and their sociability (it is hard to make a kill in the midst of a stampeding herd). They and other members of the deer family also have acquired the ability to run a little faster than wolves. Mountain goats, for their part, are able to escape up sheer cliffsides, where predators cannot trail them. Wolves have been one of the principal forces directing the evolution of these species and others, including moose, elk, bison and mountain sheep. These animals—the wolves' preferred prey—are specifically equipped to avoid wolf attacks. As the poet Robinson Jeffers once phrased it, "What but the wolf's tooth whittled so fine / The fleet limbs of the antelope"?

One not very surprising result of this relationship is that wolves are often unable to kill prey that is in prime condition. To be more accurate, they frequently do not bother to try. Biologists think that wolves evaluate their prey for weaknesses that will permit an easy kill. In the case of caribou, for example, they may "test" a herd by chasing it for a few minutes. If the prey stay bunched together and hurry nimbly away, the wolves immediately lose interest—but let one stumble or lag behind and the wolves are quick to seize the advantage. Perhaps the brief attack on the muskoxen described earlier was a similar challenge: since the animals all appeared strong, the wolves went away. In general, that is the way most wolf hunts end; available data suggest that a kill is made about one time in ten.

What are the factors that put an ungulate in this unlucky percentage? Perhaps it has an infectious disease or a severe infestation of parasites, or maybe it is hampered by injuries or age. Perhaps it is genetically inferior. Or it could be that the population has outgrown its range and the individual can't get enough to eat. In all these circumstances, it seems possible that wolves may unwittingly "benefit" their prey species by culling out the sick and the weak and helping to keep the population in check. If inferior and unproductive animals are removed, then there will be more food for healthy, well-adapted animals and their young.

Certainly, there are studies to suggest that this is often the case. On Isle Royale, in Lake Michigan, for example, moose populations crashed in the 1940s because of overpopulation and overbrowsing. But after wolves became established on the island late in that decade, moose gradually increased to about six hundred in 1960 and

fifteen hundred ten years later. David Mech, who studied the animals throughout that period, concluded that the wolves were, in fact, removing inferior animals. Although the predators were also taking a significant number of calves, they were obviously not overtaxing the moose, whose reproductive capabilities (like those of all ungulates) had a built-in allowance for such losses. These findings were in keeping with the conviction that wolves seldom adversely affect their prey species.

In recent decades, however, it has gradually become acknowledged by many biologists that the "balance of nature" is not always so evenhanded and that the effects of wolf predation on prey populations are considerably more variable and complex than at first appeared. Take the case of the Spatsizi caribou herd in northern British Columbia, for example. In the late seventies, biologists became aware that the caribou were declining because they were producing very few calves. What was going on? Were the females failing to get pregnant? No, that couldn't be the problem because, in May, almost 90 per cent of them had large udders, a sure sign that they were going to give birth. Were the newborns dying in spring storms? No, when the investigators scrambled up the mountains after the caribou in June, they found lots of big, healthy calves. Three-quarters of the cows had young. But by early July, the calves were virtually gone. They had been eaten by grizzlies, wolverine—and wolves. Although moose were also available in the area, the fresh wolf scats collected on the calving grounds contained one hundred per cent caribou. Predation appeared to be a major factor in the caribou's population decline.

Another optimistic generalization that has proven to be untrue is the contention that wolves never kill more than they need. Under most circumstances, a pack makes a kill and then returns over the succeeding days or weeks to pick the bones bare. What little they leave is cleaned up by scavengers such as ravens, eagles, foxes and lone wolves, so that nothing goes to waste. But this is not always the case. Where killing is extraordinarily easy—on caribou calving grounds or pasturelands—"surplus killing" is well documented, as it has been for other predators under similar conditions.

To some people these facts may suggest that wolves are nasty, immoral animals who ought to show more decency and a better sense of consequences. But this, of course, is foolishness. Wolves are not public servants or ecology professors; they are predators. Their "job" is killing to feed themselves and their offspring, and that is what we must expect them to do. Their impact on their prey is not limited by well-intentioned principles but is under much more effective and absolute natural control. For example, they generally don't become overly plentiful and gobble up all the available prey, because they are usually not able to do so. It is in their nature to limit their own populations. As we have seen, this is accomplished through territoriality, which restricts the number of wolves that can live in a certain area, and through the subtleties of their society, which control the number of births. Similarly, their ability to kill is restricted by their own limitations of intelligence, strength, speed and skill and by the defences of their prey. Over the long term and over large areas, their way of life remains "in balance." Otherwise they would long ago have eaten their prey and themselves into extinction.

This is true over the long term and over large areas. But in the short term and under certain local conditions, they may be capable of sending their prey and themselves into population declines, or at least of contributing to these losses. Presumably, such downward trends are often the descending curves of self-correcting natural cycles, though we humans seldom have the patience to watch them through. Suppose, for example, that a moose population suffers a succession of bad winters: too little to eat, so much deep snow that they can't escape from wolves. Their numbers begin to decrease. The spring calves, born of malnourished mothers, are also easy prey; and the downward slide accelerates. For a time, the wolves remain strong, enjoying this easy life; but eventually they too begin to run out of food and their population drops. Then, gradually, over many years, the moose and the wolves together may have a chance to build their numbers up.

So what overall effect do wolves have on their prey? Do they protect their prey populations by keeping the numbers in check, stopping the spread of disease and removing genetic weaknesses? This, as you will recall, seemed to be the case on Isle Royale. Do they take only inferior and "expendable" animals that would have died in any case—or do they actually limit and reduce their prey, as may be the case with the Spatsizi caribou? Although debate continues among the experts, the answer appears to be "all of the above." The relationship between wolves and their prey is variable and complex. It can differ from place to place, year to year, and season to season. When investigations are restricted to a local area and a short time span, definitive data and ironclad interpretations are especially hard to obtain.

It is within this mist of uncertainties that decisions about wolf control have to be made. And this is not the end of the difficulties, for there is also another factor to be taken into account, itself surrounded by a dense fog of conflicting information and emotion. This is the question of human use of animals. People are likely to be most interested in the fluctuations of animal populations if we rely on the species in some way. If, for instance, human hunters felt they had a right to the declining moose population in our example, there would inevitably be a call to reduce the number of four-legged predators. Why, the hunters might ask, should we wait through a long and uncertain natural process if we could introduce a measure of stability through appropriate management? Why let the wolves cream off all the increase in the game population if, by removing them, we could ensure a share for people?

Our recent ancestors, as we know, found ready answers to these perplexities. They simply set about eradicating wolves, not limiting or "controlling" them, but wiping them out. Except for a few throwbacks, no one would tolerate such a view today; we have seen enough genocide. We are also beginning to develop (or redevelop) a flickering awareness that other species, like ourselves, are creatures of the Earth. "Wolves, like all other wildlife, have a right to exist in a wild state," declares the manifesto on wolf conservation issued by the Wolf Specialist Group of the International Union for Conservation of Nature and Natural Resources. "This right is in no way related to their known value to mankind. Instead, it derives from the right of all living creatures to co-exist with man as part of natural ecosystems."

But if it is too brutal and stupid to claim everything for ourselves, it is too easy to say that the wolves should invariably have it all. In areas where the species is threatened or endangered, as in the northern states, wolves obviously must be given absolute priority; but where the popula-

tions are viable, as in northern Canada, we may be able to allow ourselves a few additional liberties.

Personally, I have never killed anything bigger than a fish or cuter than a mouse—I don't know how to and don't want to learn. My home is a zoo of pet birds, rodents, reptiles and dogs; when I find a bee or spider in my rooms, I carry it outdoors. I have, however, eaten many dead animals in my time; and I respect the people who raise and kill them for me. If there are individual wolves or packs that develop a tradition of taking livestock from farms and ranches, then it seems tolerable to me that those animals might be identified and killed. The zone system that has been developed in Minnesota, where government agents are permitted to kill wolves in certain tightly defined areas, also seems a reasonable solution; as do the publicly funded compensation schemes which operate in that state and in the provinces of Alberta and Ontario. If plans to restore wolves in Yellowstone and several other wilderness areas in Montana and Idaho ever proceed, both these methods are likely to be used. We must be ready, as citizens, to pay for these relatively time-consuming and expensive methods of management.

Intervention on behalf of human hunters may also be acceptable—from time to time. Suppose, for example, that a population of deer had been weakened by disease or bad weather or a poorly managed human hunt, so that the wolves, skilled opportunists to the end, were in a position to clean up on their prey. In the process, of course, they might eat themselves out of house and home and eventually clean up on themselves. We might then choose to intervene to prevent both predator and prey from hitting the bottom of this curve. Or suppose that a group of subsistence hunters were threatened with star-

vation because of some mishap to herds on which they, and the local wolf packs, relied. We might then decide that human survival—and the protection of our diminishing store of cultural diversity—were sufficiently important to justify a temporary wolf-control project.

But these are exceptional circumstances. Killing wolves should never become routine. Where control programs are proposed in the same area year after year, I think we must take it as a sign that they are not a success. Other methods should be tried instead, even if they involve limitations on recreational hunting or other human activities. We have killed enough wolves. Surely we can now, finally—after all the destruction we have brought to them—permit the survivors to live.

So how, in sum, can we live well with wolves? Obviously, there is no all-purpose, "right" way to proceed. As each new wolf-control crisis develops, difficult choices will have to be made. Ultimately, these decisions are moral and rightly involve us all. The lack of a Ph.D. is no disqualification, for these are not technical questions to be settled in closed debate by some imagined group of steel-edged, hard-eyed experts. Yes, research is crucial; we cannot think well without the best information we are able to create. But as Jacob Bronowski has pointed out, "Every judgment in science stands on the edge of error, and is personal. Science is a tribute to what we can know, although we are fallible." To live well with wolves, we must reach beyond mere information and objectivity to a more farsighted, whole-souled view that acknowledges the realities by which we live and die. Wolves challenge us to be wise.

One of the most challenging occupations of a wolf's youth is refining its skills as a hunter.

Peter J. McLeod

The ten-month-old pup at left is digging up cached food. Wolves, like red foxes, appear to have an efficient method of "bookkeeping." When a cache has been emptied, it is marked with urine. This signals that the cache is "closed" and not worth the trouble of investigating.

Peter J. McLeod

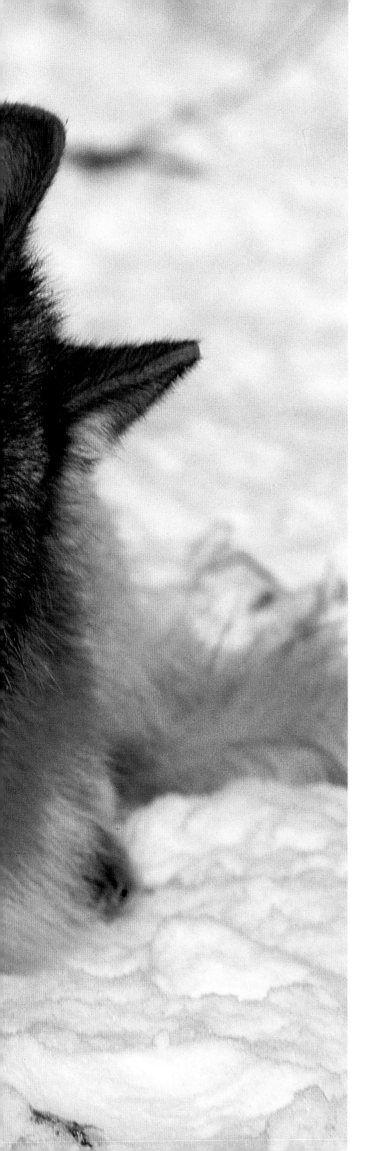

A wolf's chest is unusually narrow for a member of the dog family, permitting the animal to run with cat-like grace and efficiency.

Dennis W. Schmidt, Valan Photos

A ten-month-old pup enjoys a good chew on a stick. This may serve as a method of cleaning its teeth.

Peter J. McLeod

A wolf pack usually hunts in single-file formation.
Rolf O. Peterson

Although hoofed mammals make up most of the wolf's diet, smaller prey, including mice, hares, birds and even fish, are also on the menu. Biologist Bob Bromley once watched as a wolf caught five fish in fifteen minutes flat.

Johnny Johnson, DRK Photo

Hunting large, hoofed mammals is a dangerous livelihood. A single wolf may be able to kill an adult moose but, reciprocally, the moose may be able to kill its attacker. Beware those death-dealing front hooves! Wolves are more likely to hunt alone in the summer, when many packs temporarily split into smaller groups.

Erwin and Peggy Bauer

Its whole attention focussed on its prey, this wolf is hunting for mice.

Jim Brandenburg

Fanning out to encircle its prey, a pack of wolves prepares to attack. In this instance, the predators did not make a kill. Wolves are successful, on average, on only about ten per cent of their hunts.

Rolf O. Peterson

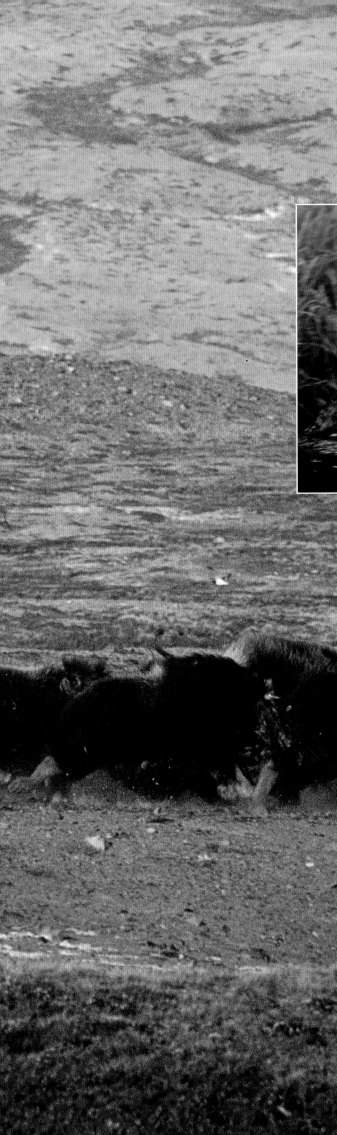

*(Inset) Dripping wet, a wolf hunts for beaver.
Thundering across the tundra, wolves test a muskox herd.*

Jim Brandenburg

Ordinarily, wolves consume their kills to the bare bones, sometimes returning over a period of several weeks to clean up the scraps.
Art Wolfe

Gathering around their kill, a pack begins to "wolf down" its prey.
Peter J. McLeod

A wolf encounters a grizzly sow and three cubs on the Toklut River in Alaska. But four to one are unappealing odds—see overleaf.

Thomas D. Mangelsen/Images of Nature®

Although the grizzly won this contest, the two species are evenly matched, and confrontations can go either way.

Thomas D. Mangelsen/Images of Nature®

Wolves often eat so much they get "meat drunk"—heavy, dazed and ready to sleep.
Thomas Kitchin, Valan Photos

Although mealtimes are irregular, sometimes days apart, each wolf requires an average of five or ten kilograms (ten or twenty pounds) of meat per day.
Peter J. McLeod

An entire pack rests on an outcrop of sun-warmed rock.
Rolf O. Peterson

In the winter, getting a drink is slow work. Wolves need plenty of water, especially after stuffing themselves at a kill.

Above, Peter J. McLeod; left, Thomas Kitchin, Valan Photos

Fed, rested and ready to run, wolves set off through the mist on a new day's hunt.

Alan D. Carey

*Wolves often take time out to play. The rules of "raven tag"
are simple—the raven sits still and within easy reach, the
wolf lunges forward, and the raven makes a last-minute
escape. Ravens who lose get eaten for lunch.*

Peter J. McLeod

*Travelling mostly in the half-light of dawn and dusk, wolves
cover an average of 15 to 25 kilometres (10 or 15 miles) each
day.*

David Hiser/Photographers Aspen

A wolf's usual playmates are other members of the pack.

Jim Brandenburg

"Want to play?" By bounding on stiffened legs, this wolf invites one of its companions to take time for a game.
Scot Stewart

Eyes wide and ears flattened to the sides, these two fun-seekers wear an expression known as the "play face."

Left, Peter J. McLeod; above, Thomas Kitchin, Valan Photos

This rack of antlers will make a fine toy on a tranquil summer morning.

Erwin and Peggy Bauer

Wolves have a right to peace.

Thomas Kitchin, Valan Photos

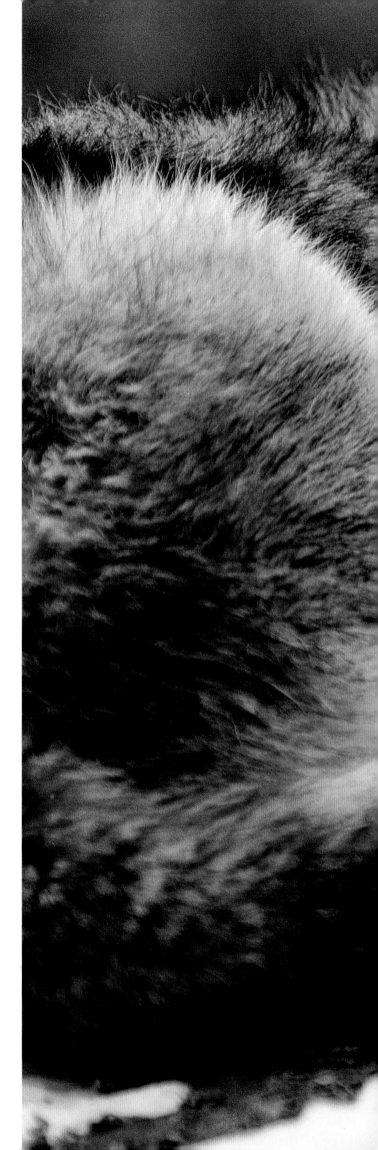

Encountered face to face, wolves are very different than many of us have supposed. Intelligence, friendliness and curiosity are amongst the species' foremost qualities.

Michael Ederegger, DRK Photo

A wolf emerging from moist green woods in Denali National Park, Alaska, surprises us with its beauty.

Erwin and Peggy Bauer

Wolves are keepers of the wild. We have a right to their company.

Heather Parr Fentress

R E F E R E N C E S

The literature on wolves is vast. A computer search of the standard scientific sources reveals 18,000 separate

titles on the subject of *Canis lupus.* This listing, therefore, is necessarily selective.

In addition to written information, several interesting films are available. One of the best is a 44-minute production entitled *Following the Tundra Wolf,* which can be obtained from the Visual Education Centre, 15 Horner Avenue, unit 1, Toronto, Ontario M8Z 4X5. Other interesting titles include *Wolf Pack,* a 20-minute production by Canadian Bill Mason, available from the National Film Board, and *Wild Dogs of Jasper,* a 25-minute work from Karvonen Productions of Sherwood Park, Alberta.

Ballard, Warren B; Whitman, Jackson S.; and Gardner, Craig L. 1987. "Ecology of an exploited wolf population in south-central Alaska." *Wildlife Monographs* 98.

Bergerud, A. T.; Wyett, W.; and Snider, B. 1983. "The role of wolf predation in limiting a moose population." *Journal of Wildlife Management* 47:977–88.

Bromley, Robert G. 1973. "Fishing behavior of a wolf on the Taltson River, Northwest Territories." *Canadian Field-Naturalist* 87:301–303.

Bronowski, Jacob. 1973. *The ascent of man.* Boston: Little Brown.

Carbyn, Ludwig N. 1983a. "Management of non-endangered wolf populations in Canada." *Acta Zool. Fennica* 174:239–43.

———— 1983b. "Wolf predation on elk in Riding Mountain National Park, Manitoba." *Journal of Wildlife Management* 47:963–76.

————. 1983c. *Wolves in Canada and Alaska.* Canadian Wildlife Service Report Series, No. 25.

————. 1981. "Territory displacement in a wolf population with abundant prey." *Journal of Mammalogy* 62:193–95.

————. 1974. "Wolf population fluctuations in Jasper National Park, Alberta, Canada." *Biological Conservation* 6:94–101.

Cowan, Ian McTaggart. 1947. "The timber wolf in the Rocky Mountain National Parks of Canada." *Canadian Journal of Research* 25 (sec. D): 139–74.

Crisler, Lois. 1958. *Arctic wild.* New York: Harper and Brothers.

Decker, Daniel J., and Brown, Tommy L. 1987. "How animal rightests view the 'wildlife management-hunting system.'" *Wildlife Society Bulletin* 15:599–602.

Fritts, Steven H.; Paul, William J.; and Mech, L. David. 1985. "Can relocated wolves survive?" *Wildlife Society Bulletin* 13:459–63.

Gray, David R. 1987. *The muskoxen of Polar Bear Pass*. Toronto: Fitzhenry and Whiteside.

Hall, Roberta L., and Sharp, Henry S., eds. 1978. *Wolf and man: evolution in parallel*. New York: Academic Press.

Harrington, Fred H. 1981. "Urine-marking and caching behaviour in the wolf." *Behaviour* 76:280–88.

Harrington, Fred H., and Mech, L. David. 1983. "Wolf pack spacing: howling as a territory-independent spacing mechanism in a territorial population." *Behavioral Ecology and Sociobiology* 12:161–68.

Harrington, Fred H., Mech, L. David; and Fritts, Steven H. 1983. "Pack size and wolf pup survival: their relationship under varying ecological conditions." *Behavioral Ecology and Sociobiology* 13:19–26.

Harrington, Fred H., and Paquet, Paul C., eds. 1982. *Wolves of the world: perspectives of behavior, ecology, and conservation*. Park Ridge, N.J.: Noyes Publications.

Heard, Douglas C. 1984. "Historical and present status of wolves in the Northwest Territories." Northwest Territories Renewable Resources Information Series Report No. 4.

Heard, D. C.; Sleck, E. S.; and Calef, G. W. "The wolf on the barren grounds in central Northwest Territories." Unpublished manuscript.

Henriksen, Georg. 1973. *Hunters in the barrens: the Naskapi on the edge of the white man's world*. St. John's: Memorial University of Newfoundland.

Jenness, Stuart E. 1985. "Arctic wolf attacks scientist—a unique Canadian incident." *Arctic* 38:129–32.

Joslin, Paul W. B. 1967. "Movements and home sites of timber wolves in Algonquin Park." *American Zoologist* 7:279–88.

Klinghammer, Erich, ed. 1979. *The behavior and ecology of wolves*. Proceedings of a symposium on the behavior and ecology of wolves, 23–24 May 1975. New York: Garlan STPM Press.

Kuyt, E. 1962. "Movements of young wolves in the Northwest Territories of Canada." *Journal of Mammalogy* 43:270–71.

Lidle, Janet, ed. 1986; 1987. *Wolf!* (An independent quarterly newsletter, committed to the survival of the wolf in the wild and its welfare in captivity.) Vol. 4(3); Vol. 5(1–4).

Linderman, Frank B. 1957. *American: the life story of a great Indian, Plenty-Coups, chief of the Crows*. New York: Harper and Row.

Lopez, Barry. 1978. *Of wolves and men*. New York: Charles Scribner's Sons.

Mair, W. W., and Banfield, A. W. F. 1956. The wolf control program in the Northwest Territories. Canadian Wildlife Service. Unpublished report.

Mary-Rousseliere, Guy, o.m.i. 1987. "How old Monica Ataguttaaluk introduced me to Arctic archaeology." *Inuktitut* 66:6–24.

McNaught, David A. 1987. "Wolves in Yellowstone?—park visitors respond." *Wildlife Society Bulletin* 15:518–20.

Mech, L. David. 1987. "At home with the arctic wolf." *National Geographic* (May): 562–92.

———. 1977. "Wolf-pack buffer zones as prey reservoirs." *Science* 198:320–21.

———. 1970. *The wolf: the ecology and behavior of an endangered species*. Garden City, N.Y.: American Museum of Natural History and Natural History Press.

———. 1966. *The wolves of Isle Royale*. Fauna of the National Parks of the United States, Fauna Series 7.

Messier, François, and Crete, Michel. 1985. "Moose-wolf dynamics and the natural regulation of moose populations." *Oecologia* 65:503–12.

Miller, D. R. 1975. "Observations of wolf predation on barren ground caribou in winter." *First international reindeer and caribou symposium*. In Jack R. Luick et al., eds. Biological Papers of the University of Alaska. Special Report No. 1, pp. 209–20.

Miller, Frank L.; Gunn, Anne; and Broughton, Eric. 1985. "Surplus killing as exemplified by wolf predation on newborn caribou." *Canadian Journal of Zoology* 63:295–300.

Mowat, Farley. 1983. *Never cry wolf*. Toronto: Seal Books, McClelland and Stewart—Bantam.

Murie, Adolph. 1971 (reprint of 1944 edition). *The*

wolves of Mount McKinley. Fauna of the National Parks of the United States, Fauna Series No. 5.

Nelson, Michael E., and Mech, L. David. 1985. "Observation of a wolf killed by a deer." *Journal of Mammalogy* 66:187–88.

Neumann, Erich. 1963. *The great mother: an analysis of the archetype*. Princeton, N.J.: Princeton University Press, Bollingen Series.

Obee, Bruce. 1984. "Wolves of British Columbia: predator or prey?" *Wildlife Review* (summer): 5–25.

Packard, Jane M., and Mech, L. David. 1980. "Population regulation in wolves." In M. N. Cohen et al., eds. *Biosocial mechanisms of population regulation*. New Haven: Yale University Press, pp. 135–50.

Peterson, Rolf O. 1977. *Wolf ecology and prey relationships on Isle Royale*. National Park Service Scientific Monograph Series 11.

Pimlott, Douglas H. 1961. "Wolf control in Canada." Reprinted from *Canadian Audubon Magazine*, Nov.–Dec. 1961, by Canadian Wildlife Service.

Pisano, Robert. 1977. "The status of the wolf in North America." International Society for the Protection of Animals, Scientific Series No. 2.

Rabb, George B.; Woolpy, Jerome H.; and Ginsburg, Benson E. 1967. "Social relationships in a group of captive wolves." *American Zoologist* 7:305–11.

Ramsay, M. A., and Seip, D. R., eds. 1979. "Symposium on wolf predation." Simon Fraser University, December 1, 1978.

Savage, Arthur, and Savage, Candace. 1981. *Wild mammals of Western Canada*. Saskatoon, Sask.: Western Producer Prairie Books.

Schenkel, Rudolf. 1967. "Submission: its features and function in the wolf and dog." *American Zoologist* 7:319–29.

Schmidt, Joel. 1980. *Larousse Greek and Roman mythology*. New York: McGraw-Hill.

Theberge, John B. 1975. *Wolves and wilderness*. Toronto: Dent.

Theberge, John B., and Falls, J. Bruce. 1967. "Howling as a means of communication in timber wolves." *American Zoologist* 7:331–38.

Walker, Barbara G. 1983. *The woman's encyclopedia of myths and secrets*. San Francisco: Harper and Row.

Wolves in American Culture Committee. 1986. *Wolf!* Ashland, Wisconsin: NorthWord.

Woolpy, Jerome H., and Ginsburg, Benson E. 1967. "Wolf socialization: a study of temperament in a wild social species." *American Zoologist* 7:357–63.

Zimen, Erik. 1981. *The wolf: his place in the natural world*. London: Souvenir Press.